THE EASY AIP COOKBOOK

Simple Recipes for a Delicious and Healthy Lifestyle

Debra D. Gemmil

Copyright© Debra D. Gemmil, 2024

All rights reserved.

Without the author's express written consent, no portion of this book may be copied or transmitted in any way, whether it be electronically or mechanically, including by photocopying, recording, or information storing and retrieval systems.

TABLE OF CONTENT

Embracing the Easy AIP: Your Flavorful Journey to Healing 7

- What's the AIP All About? 7
- Why Should You Care? 7
- The Science of Healing 7
- Busting AIP Myths 8
- Shopping for AIP Success 9
- Foods to Avoid 10
- General Substitutions 10
- Recipe-Specific Substitutions 10

Beginner AIP Meal Plan (2 Weeks) 12

Experienced AIP Meal Plan (2 Weeks) 13

Breakfast 16

- Sweet Potato & Apple Breakfast Hash: A Cozy Start to Your Day 16
- Coconut Flour Pancakes: A Fluffy and Flavorful AIP Delight 18
- Breakfast Sausage Egg Muffins: Bite-Sized Flavor Bombs 20
- Plantain Porridge: A Warm & Creamy AIP Breakfast 22
- Green Dream AIP Smoothie: A Vibrant Start to Your Day 24
- Salmon Cakes with Avocado Salsa: A Fiesta of Flavor 26
- Zucchini Fritters: Crispy Golden Bites of summer 28
- Chicken Apple Sausage Hash: Hearty & Wholesome 29

AIP Breakfast Bowl: Nourishing & Vibrant 30

AIP Banana Bread: A Sweet and Satisfying Treat 31

Lunch 33

Turkey Lettuce Wraps: A Flavorful & Fun AIP Meal 33

Carrot Ginger Soup: A Warming Embrace in a Bowl 35

Chicken Salad with Avocado Mayo: A Creamy & Refreshing AIP Lunch 37

Sweet Potato & Kale Salad: A Vibrant Symphony of Fall Flavors 39

Leftover Roasted Chicken & Veggie Bowls: Flavorful Fuel in a Flash 41

AIP Zucchini Noodles with Nomato Sauce: A Flavorful & Comforting Dish 42

Nourishing Chicken Soup: Your AIP Comfort in a Bowl 44

Avocado Tuna Salad: A Creamy & Flavorful AIP Delight 46

Cauliflower Rice Stir-Fry: A Rainbow of Flavors & Textures (AIP-Friendly) 48

Salmon Salad with Lemon-Dill Dressing: A Light & Zesty AIP Meal 50

Dinner 52

Lemon Herb Baked Chicken: A Simple & Flavorful AIP Staple 52

AIP Shepherd's Pie: Comfort Food with a Healing Twist 54

Baked Salmon with Roasted Vegetables: A Nourishing Symphony of Flavors 56

Slow Cooker Beef Stew: Comforting & Flavorful AIP Goodness 58

Shrimp Scampi with Zucchini Noodles: A Light & Zesty AIP Feast 60

Turkey Meatballs in Nomato Sauce: AIP Comfort Food at Its Best 62

Pork Chops with Caramelized Apples & Onions: A Sweet & Savory AIP Delight 64

AIP Chicken Curry: A Warm & Fragrant Bowl of Comfort 65

Roasted Butternut Squash Soup: Autumn in a Bowl (AIP-Friendly) 67

Beef and Broccoli Stir-Fry: A Flavorful AIP Classic 68

Snacks 70

Fruit with Almond Butter (AIP Reintroduction Phase): A Simple & Satisfying Snack ... 70

Veggie Sticks with Guacamole: A Fiesta of Freshness (AIP-Friendly) 72

Hard-Boiled Eggs (AIP Reintroduction Phase): Protein Powerhouses in a Shell 73

Baked Plantain Chips: A Crispy & Savory AIP Snack 74

Rainbow Fruit Salad: A Burst of AIP-Friendly Sunshine 75

Coconut Yogurt with Berries: A Tropical Delight (AIP-Friendly) 76

Carrot Sticks with "No-Chickpea" Hummus: A Crunchy & Flavorful AIP Snack 78

Baked Sweet Potato Chips: A Sweet & Savory AIP Snack 79

Avocado Deviled Eggs: A Creamy & Flavorful AIP Appetizer 80

Ants on a Log" (AIP-Friendly): A Crunchy & Fun Snack 82

Soups & Stews 84

Creamy Carrot & Ginger Soup: A Warming Hug for Your Soul (AIP-Friendly) 84

Chicken Zoodle Soup: Nourishing & Flavorful AIP Comfort 85

Roasted Butternut Squash Soup: Autumn in a Bowl (AIP-Friendly) 87

Crockpot Beef Stew: Comforting Warmth Made Easy (AIP-Friendly) 88

Hearty Turkey Vegetable Soup: Comforting & Nourishing AIP Goodness 89

Curried Cauliflower Soup: A Flavorful and Aromatic AIP Delight 91

Broccoli and Kale Soup: A Vibrant & Nourishing AIP Elixir 93

Chicken and Sweet Potato Chowder: A Creamy, AIP-Friendly Comfort 95

AIP Pumpkin Chili: A Warm & Cozy Fall Favorite 96

AIP French Onion Soup: Savory Comfort, Simplified 98

Sides 100

AIP Mashed Sweet Potatoes: A Silky & Satisfying Side Dish 100

Garlic Green Beans: Simple, Savory, & AIP-Approved 102

Roasted Brussels sprouts with Bacon: Crispy, Savory, & AIP-Approved 103

Baked Carrot Fries: A Crispy & Flavorful AIP Snack 104

AIP Broccoli Salad: Crunchy, Creamy, and Refreshing 105

AIP Mashed Cauliflower: A Cloud of Comfort (Dairy-Free & Delicious) 106

Sautéed Kale with Garlic: A Nutrient-Rich AIP Side Dish 108

Desserts & Sweets 110

AIP Coconut Flour Brownies: Fudgy, Decadent, and Healing 110

AIP Coconut Flour Brownies: Fudgy, Decadent, and Healing 111

AIP Banana Nice Cream: A Naturally Sweet & Creamy Frozen Treat 112

Mango Sorbet: A Tropical Twist on a Refreshing Treat (AIP-Friendly) 113

AIP Apple Crisp: Warm & Comforting Autumnal Bliss 114

AIP Chocolate Avocado Pudding: Decadent & Guilt-Free 116

AIP Coconut Milk Ice Cream: Tropical & Refreshing 116

AIP Pumpkin Spice Muffins: Warm & Cozy Fall Treats 117

Strawberry Chia Seed Pudding: A Refreshing & Nutritious AIP Treat 118

AIP Carrot Cake Muffins: Warm & Spiced Treats 119

Embracing the Easy AIP: Your Flavorful Journey to Healing

Let's face it, dealing with an autoimmune condition can feel like a culinary minefield. Every meal becomes a guessing game of "Will this make me flare?" But what if I told you that eating delicious food could actually be a powerful tool in your healing arsenal?

That's where the Autoimmune Protocol (AIP) comes in.

What's the AIP All About?

Imagine giving your body a much-needed vacation from foods that might be triggering inflammation and wreaking havoc on your immune system. The AIP is like a reset button, eliminating common culprits like grains, dairy, legumes, nightshades, and processed foods for a period of time. It's not just about saying "no" to certain foods, though. It's about saying a resounding "yes!" to nutrient-dense, whole foods that nourish your body and promote healing.

Why Should You Care?

Picture this: I was diagnosed with Hashimoto's thyroiditis a few years ago, and my energy levels plummeted. Fatigue became my constant companion, brain fog clouded my thoughts, and my joints ached. It felt like my body was betraying me. But then I discovered AIP. It wasn't an overnight miracle, but slowly and surely, I felt my energy return, my brain fog lift, and my pain subside. I rediscovered my love for cooking and found that AIP wasn't about deprivation—it was about abundance.

The Science of Healing

You might be wondering, "Does this actually work?" The exciting news is that there's growing scientific evidence supporting the benefits of AIP for autoimmune conditions. It's not just anecdotal; research suggests that AIP can:

- Reduce inflammation: By eliminating potential trigger foods, AIP helps calm the immune response and reduce chronic inflammation, a hallmark of autoimmune diseases.

- Heal the gut: A leaky gut allows harmful substances to enter the bloodstream, potentially worsening autoimmune symptoms. AIP focuses on gut-healing foods to restore its integrity.
- Improve nutrient status: AIP emphasizes nutrient-dense foods, ensuring you get the vitamins, minerals, and antioxidants your body needs to thrive.

Busting AIP Myths

- Myth 1: "AIP is too restrictive!"
    - Reality: While the initial elimination phase is strict, it's temporary. Once you identify your trigger foods, you can gradually reintroduce some back into your diet. Plus, AIP offers a world of delicious and creative possibilities, so your taste buds won't be bored!
- Myth 2: "I'll have to cook all my meals from scratch."
    - Reality: While cooking at home is encouraged, there are plenty of AIP-compliant convenience foods and pre-made meals available. It's about finding a balance that works for you.
- Myth 3: "AIP is expensive!"
    - Reality: It's true that some specialty AIP products can be pricey, but you can focus on affordable staples like vegetables, fruits, and meat. Planning and prepping meals in advance can also help save money.

This cookbook is your guide to embracing the Easy AIP lifestyle. Together, we'll explore simple, flavorful recipes that make healing your body a delicious and enjoyable experience. So, grab your apron, let's get cooking, and reclaim your health one delicious bite at a time!

Your Easy AIP Adventure Begins: A Beginner's Guide You've decided to embark on an exciting culinary journey with the Autoimmune Protocol (AIP). Congratulations! This is a huge step towards reclaiming your health and well-being. To make your transition as smooth and enjoyable as possible, let's dive into a step-by-step guide filled with practical tips, helpful resources, and a dash of personal experience.

Step 1: Embrace the Mindset

The first step to AIP success isn't about stocking your pantry; it's about embracing a new mindset. Think of this as an opportunity to nourish your body, discover new flavors, and reconnect with your inner chef.

- **Be patient:** Changing your diet takes time and effort. Don't get discouraged if you slip up or have a bad day. Remember, progress is more important than perfection.
- **Be kind to yourself:** It's normal to experience cravings and emotional ups and downs. Acknowledge your feelings and find healthy ways to cope.
- **Celebrate small victories:** Every AIP-compliant meal is a win! Celebrate your progress and focus on the positive changes you're making.

Step 2: Clean Out Your Kitchen

It's time to say goodbye to old habits and clear out your kitchen of non-AIP foods. This might feel daunting, but it's a crucial step in setting yourself up for success.

- **Donate or discard:** Non-compliant foods like grains, legumes, dairy, nightshades, processed foods, and refined sugars.
- **Stock up:** Fill your pantry and fridge with AIP-friendly staples like vegetables, fruits, meat, fish, healthy fats, and herbs and spices.

Step 3: Meal Planning Made Easy

Planning your meals in advance is a game-changer when it comes to sticking to AIP. It helps you stay on track, avoid last-minute temptations, and save time and money.

- **Start simple:** Begin with easy recipes that use familiar ingredients. As you gain confidence, you can experiment with more complex dishes.
- **Prep ahead:** Chop vegetables, cook proteins, and make sauces on the weekends to streamline your weekday cooking.
- **Cook in batches:** Double or triple recipes and freeze leftovers for later.

Shopping for AIP Success

Knowing what to buy at the grocery store can be overwhelming at first. Here's a cheat sheet of AIP-compliant foods to stock up on:

- **Vegetables:** All vegetables (except nightshades)
- **Fruits:** All fruits (in moderation)
- **Meat & Poultry:** Grass-fed, pasture-raised options
- **Fish & Seafood:** Wild-caught varieties
- **Healthy Fats:** Avocado oil, coconut oil, olive oil, ghee, nuts, and seeds (reintroduce cautiously)

- **Herbs & Spices:** All fresh and dried herbs and spices

Foods to Avoid

- Grains: Wheat, rice, oats, quinoa, corn, etc.
- Legumes: Beans, lentils, peanuts, peas
- Dairy: Milk, cheese, yogurt, butter
- Nightshades: Tomatoes, potatoes, peppers, eggplant
- Eggs: (reintroduce cautiously)
- Nuts & Seeds: (reintroduce cautiously)
- Processed Foods: Anything with added sugar, artificial ingredients, or preservatives
- Refined Sugar: White sugar, brown sugar, agave, maple syrup
- Alcohol

General Substitutions

- **Nightshades (tomatoes, peppers, eggplant):** Replace with carrots, beets, sweet potatoes, butternut squash, or other AIP-compliant vegetables for similar flavors and colors.
- **Eggs:** Substitute with mashed bananas or applesauce for binding in baked goods or try silken tofu or mashed avocado for creaminess in dips and sauces.
- **Nuts and seeds:** Use shredded coconut, sunflower seed butter (if tolerated), or mashed sweet potato for a similar texture and flavor profile.
- **Dairy:** Substitute with coconut milk, coconut cream, or coconut yogurt for creaminess in sauces and desserts.
- **Grains:** Use cauliflower rice, sweet potato "toast," or mashed plantains as a base for meals.

Recipe-Specific Substitutions

- **Chicken Apple Sausage Hash:** Instead of apples, use chopped pears or peaches for sweetness.
- **Zucchini Noodles with Meat Sauce:** Use mashed winter squash or sweet potatoes instead of tomatoes in the sauce.
- **Roasted Brussels Sprouts with Bacon:** Omit the balsamic glaze or replace it with a drizzle of honey or maple syrup.
- **Broccoli Salad:** Use mashed avocado instead of mayonnaise in the dressing.

- **AIP Chocolate Avocado Pudding:** Omit or replace nuts with shredded coconut or sunflower seed butter (if tolerated).
- **AIP Pumpkin Spice Muffins:** You can use mashed bananas or applesauce instead of eggs for a binder.
- **Ants on a Log:** Use mashed banana or sweet potato with coconut butter as a filling instead of almond butter and raisins.

Important Note:

Always double-check all ingredients for AIP compliance, as some brands may contain hidden non-compliant ingredients. Look for labels that specifically state "AIP-friendly" or "Paleo Autoimmune Protocol."

Remember, the elimination phase is temporary. As you progress through the AIP diet and reintroduce foods, you'll be able to enjoy a wider variety of ingredients and flavors.

Beginner AIP Meal Plan (2 Weeks)

Week 1:

- Day 1:
    - Breakfast: Sweet Potato & Apple Breakfast Hash
    - Lunch: Leftover Roasted Chicken & Veggie Bowls
    - Dinner: Lemon Herb Baked Chicken with Roasted Vegetables
    - Snack: Fruit with Almond Butter
- Day 2:
    - Breakfast: Coconut Flour Pancakes
    - Lunch: Chicken Salad with Avocado Mayo
    - Dinner: Slow Cooker Beef Stew
    - Snack: Veggie Sticks with Guacamole
- Day 3:
    - Breakfast: Breakfast Sausage Egg Muffins
    - Lunch: Leftover Slow Cooker Beef Stew
    - Dinner: Turkey Meatballs in Tomato Sauce with Zucchini Noodles
    - Snack: Plantain Chips
- Day 4:
    - Breakfast: AIP Smoothie
    - Lunch: Leftover Turkey Meatballs in Tomato Sauce with Zucchini Noodles
    - Dinner: Salmon with Roasted Vegetables
    - Snack: Fruit Salad
- Day 5:
    - Breakfast: Sweet Potato & Apple Breakfast Hash
    - Lunch: Salmon Salad with Lemon-Dill Dressing
    - Dinner: Chicken Soup
    - Snack: Carrot Sticks with Hummus
- **Day 6 & 7:** Repeat or choose your favorite meals from the week.

Week 2:

- Day 1:
    - Breakfast: Plantain Porridge
    - Lunch: Leftover Chicken Soup
    - Dinner: Pork Chops with Apples and Onions
    - Snack: Hard-Boiled Eggs

- Day 2:
    - Breakfast: Coconut Flour Pancakes
    - Lunch: Sweet Potato & Kale Salad
    - Dinner: Shrimp Scampi with Zucchini Noodles
    - Snack: Coconut Yogurt with Berries
- Day 3:
    - Breakfast: Breakfast Sausage Egg Muffins
    - Lunch: Leftover Shrimp Scampi with Zucchini Noodles
    - Dinner: Lemon Herb Baked Chicken with Roasted Vegetables
    - Snack: Sweet Potato Chips
- Day 4:
    - Breakfast: AIP Smoothie
    - Lunch: Leftover Lemon Herb Baked Chicken with Roasted Vegetables
    - Dinner: Beef and Broccoli Stir-Fry
    - Snack: Fruit with Almond Butter
- Day 5:
    - Breakfast: Sweet Potato & Apple Breakfast Hash
    - Lunch: Leftover Beef and Broccoli Stir-Fry
    - Dinner: Salmon with Roasted Vegetables
    - Snack: Veggie Sticks with Guacamole
- **Day 6 & 7:** Repeat or choose your favorite meals from the week.

Experienced AIP Meal Plan (2 Weeks)

Week 1:

- Day 1:
    - Breakfast: Plantain Porridge with Berries
    - Lunch: Zucchini Noodles with Meat Sauce
    - Dinner: Salmon with Roasted Vegetables and Cauliflower Rice
    - Snack: Avocado Deviled Eggs
- Day 2:
    - Breakfast: AIP Breakfast Bowl with Poached Egg
    - Lunch: Leftover Zucchini Noodles with Meat Sauce
    - Dinner: Slow Cooker Beef Stew with Mashed Cauliflower
    - Snack: Ants on a Log
- Day 3:

- Breakfast: Salmon Cakes with Avocado Salsa
- Lunch: Leftover Slow Cooker Beef Stew
- Dinner: Turkey Meatballs in Tomato Sauce with Spiralized Sweet Potato Noodles
- Snack: Fruit Salad with Coconut Flakes
- Day 4:
    - Breakfast: AIP Smoothie with Collagen Peptides
    - Lunch: Leftover Turkey Meatballs with Spiralized Sweet Potato Noodles
    - Dinner: Chicken Curry with Coconut Milk and Cauliflower Rice
    - Snack: Carrot Fries with AIP-friendly dipping sauce
- Day 5:
    - Breakfast: Zucchini Fritters with Avocado and Lime
    - Lunch: Chicken Salad with Avocado Mayo and Plantain Chips
    - Dinner: Roasted Butternut Squash Soup
    - Snack: Sweet Potato Chips with Guacamole
- **Day 6 & 7:** Repeat or choose favorite meals from the week, incorporating new recipes as desired.

Week 2:

- Day 1:
    - Breakfast: Plantain Pancakes with Cinnamon and Berries
    - Lunch: Leftover Roasted Butternut Squash Soup
    - Dinner: Pork Chops with Caramelized Apples and Onions, served with Roasted Brussels Sprouts and Bacon
    - Snack: Mixed Nuts and Seeds (if tolerated)
- Day 2:
    - Breakfast: AIP Breakfast Bowl with Sautéed Mushrooms and Greens
    - Lunch: Leftover Pork Chops and Roasted Brussels Sprouts
    - Dinner: Shrimp Scampi with Zucchini Noodles and Garlic-Lemon Sauce
    - Snack: Plantain Chips with Guacamole
- Day 3:
    - Breakfast: Chicken Apple Sausage Hash
    - Lunch: Leftover Shrimp Scampi
    - Dinner: Beef and Broccoli Stir-Fry with Cauliflower Rice
    - Snack: Carrot Sticks and Hummus
- Day 4:
    - Breakfast: AIP Smoothie with added Protein Powder

- Lunch: Leftover Beef and Broccoli Stir-Fry
- Dinner: Salmon with Roasted Vegetables and a side of Sautéed Kale with Garlic
- Snack: Banana Nice Cream
- Day 5:
  - Breakfast: Sweet Potato and Apple Hash with a side of Avocado
  - Lunch: Salad with leftover Salmon, mixed greens, avocado, and a Lemon-Dill dressing
  - Dinner: Chicken Curry with Coconut Milk and Cauliflower Rice
  - Snack: Fruit Salad with Coconut Flakes
- **Day 6 & 7:** Repeat favorite meals, experiment with new AIP recipes, or enjoy a meal out at an AIP-friendly restaurant.

Breakfast

"Let food be thy medicine and medicine be thy food." - Hippocrates

Sweet Potato & Apple Breakfast Hash: A Cozy Start to Your Day

Prep Time: 15 minutes **Cook Time:** 30 minutes **Yields:** 4 servings

This hearty and flavorful hash is the perfect way to start your day on the AIP diet. The combination of sweet potatoes, apples, sausage, and warm spices creates a satisfying and nutritious breakfast that will keep you feeling full and energized.

Ingredients:

- 1 pound breakfast sausage (AIP-compliant, no sugar or nightshades)
- 2 medium sweet potatoes, peeled and diced
- 2 apples (Honeycrisp or Granny Smith), diced
- 1/2 medium yellow onion, diced
- 2 cloves garlic, minced
- 1 tablespoon avocado oil or ghee
- 1 teaspoon ground cinnamon
- 1/2 teaspoon ground nutmeg
- 1/4 teaspoon ground ginger
- 1/4 teaspoon salt
- 1/4 teaspoon black pepper
- Fresh chopped herbs (parsley, thyme, or rosemary), for garnish

Instructions:

1. In a large skillet over medium heat, cook the breakfast sausage until browned and cooked through. Break it into smaller pieces as it cooks. Remove the sausage from the skillet and set aside.
2. In the same skillet, heat the avocado oil or ghee over medium heat. Add the diced sweet potatoes and apples, and cook for about 10 minutes, or until they begin to soften.
3. Add the diced onion and minced garlic to the skillet. Cook for another 5 minutes, or until the onions are translucent.
4. Return the cooked sausage to the skillet.
5. Stir in the cinnamon, nutmeg, ginger, salt, and pepper. Cook for an additional 5 minutes, or until the flavors are well combined.
6. Serve the Sweet Potato & Apple Breakfast Hash warm, garnished with fresh chopped herbs.

Tips:

- For extra flavor, add a tablespoon of apple cider vinegar to the skillet along with the spices.
- If you prefer a crispy hash, cook the sweet potatoes and apples for a few extra minutes until they begin to brown.
- You can also add chopped greens like kale or spinach to the hash for added nutrients.

I remember the first time I made this hash for my family. My son, who is notoriously picky about vegetables, took one bite and declared it "the best breakfast ever!" It's become a regular part of our weekend brunch rotation, and it's always a hit.

Enjoy this delicious and nutritious Sweet Potato & Apple Breakfast Hash, and feel good knowing you're nourishing your body with wholesome, AIP-compliant ingredients. Here's to a happy and healthy start to your day!

"Eating healthy food fills your body with energy and nutrients. Imagine your cells smiling back at you and saying: 'Thank you!'" - Karen Salmansohn

Coconut Flour Pancakes: A Fluffy and Flavorful AIP Delight

Prep Time: 5 minutes **Cook Time:** 10 minutes **Yields:** 6-8 pancakes

These light and fluffy pancakes are a delicious and satisfying way to start your day on the AIP diet. Made with simple, wholesome ingredients like coconut flour, banana, and coconut milk, they're packed with nutrients and free of common allergens.

Ingredients:

- 1/2 cup coconut flour
- 1/4 teaspoon baking soda
- 1/4 teaspoon salt
- 4 large eggs
- 1 ripe banana, mashed
- 1/2 cup full-fat coconut milk
- 1 tablespoon honey or maple syrup (optional)
- 1 teaspoon vanilla extract
- Ghee or coconut oil, for cooking

Instructions:

1. In a large bowl, whisk together the coconut flour, baking soda, and salt.
2. In a separate bowl, whisk together the eggs, mashed banana, coconut milk, honey (if using), and vanilla extract.
3. Pour the wet ingredients into the dry ingredients and whisk until just combined. Don't overmix, as this can make the pancakes tough.
4. Heat a large skillet or griddle over medium heat. Grease lightly with ghee or coconut oil.
5. Pour 1/4 cup of batter onto the skillet for each pancake. Cook for 2-3 minutes per side, or until golden brown and cooked through.
6. Serve warm with your favorite AIP-compliant toppings, such as berries, sliced bananas, coconut flakes, or a drizzle of honey or maple syrup.

Tips:

- If the batter is too thick, add a tablespoon or two of extra coconut milk until it reaches a pourable consistency.
- For extra fluffy pancakes, let the batter rest for 5-10 minutes before cooking.
- To make the pancakes nut-free, omit the almond flour.
- To make the pancakes egg-free, try substituting 1/4 cup of applesauce for each egg.

I used to think pancakes were off-limits on AIP, but this recipe changed everything! I love how simple they are to make, and the addition of banana gives them a subtle sweetness that satisfies my cravings.

Enjoy these fluffy and delicious Coconut Flour Pancakes as a nutritious and satisfying start to your day on the AIP diet!

"Eating healthy doesn't have to be boring. With a little creativity, you can make delicious and nutritious meals that fuel your body and soul." – Unknown

Breakfast Sausage Egg Muffins: Bite-Sized Flavor Bombs

Prep Time: 10 minutes **Cook Time:** 20 minutes **Yields:** 12 muffins

These protein-packed, veggie-filled breakfast sausage egg muffins are a delicious and convenient way to start your day on the AIP diet. They're perfect for meal prep, on-the-go breakfasts, or a quick and easy brunch option.

Ingredients:

- 1 pound breakfast sausage (AIP-compliant, no sugar or nightshades)
- 1/2 medium yellow onion, diced
- 1 bell pepper (any color), diced
- 1 zucchini, diced
- 1 cup chopped spinach or kale
- 6 large eggs
- 1/4 cup full-fat coconut milk
- 1/2 teaspoon salt
- 1/4 teaspoon black pepper
- 1/4 teaspoon dried oregano
- 1/4 teaspoon dried thyme

Instructions:

1. Preheat oven to 375°F (190°C). Grease a 12-cup muffin tin with avocado oil or ghee.
2. In a large skillet over medium heat, cook the breakfast sausage until browned and cooked through. Break it into smaller pieces as it cooks.
3. Add the diced onion, bell pepper, and zucchini to the skillet with the sausage. Cook for 5-7 minutes, or until the vegetables are softened.
4. Stir in the chopped spinach or kale and cook for an additional 2-3 minutes, or until wilted.
5. In a large bowl, whisk together the eggs, coconut milk, salt, pepper, oregano, and thyme.
6. Divide the sausage and vegetable mixture evenly among the muffin cups.
7. Pour the egg mixture over the sausage and vegetable mixture, filling each cup about 3/4 full.
8. Bake for 18-20 minutes, or until the muffins are set and golden brown.
9. Let the muffins cool in the tin for a few minutes before removing. Serve warm or at room temperature.

Tips:

- For a spicy kick, add a pinch of red pepper flakes to the egg mixture.
- Feel free to substitute other AIP-compliant vegetables, such as broccoli florets, cauliflower florets, or mushrooms.
- These muffins can be stored in the refrigerator for up to 5 days or frozen for up to 3 months.

I used to struggle with finding quick and easy AIP breakfast options, but these egg muffins are a lifesaver! I love that I can make a batch ahead of time and have a healthy and delicious breakfast ready to go whenever I need it.

Enjoy these flavorful and satisfying Breakfast Sausage Egg Muffins, knowing they're a perfect addition to your AIP lifestyle!

"Breakfast is everything. The beginning, the first thing. It is the mouthful that is the commitment to a new day, a continuing life." – A.A. Gill

Plantain Porridge: A Warm & Creamy AIP Breakfast

Prep Time: 5 minutes **Cook Time:** 15 minutes **Yields:** 2 servings

This creamy and naturally sweet porridge is a satisfying and nourishing way to start your day on the AIP diet. Made with ripe plantains, coconut milk, and warming spices, it's a delicious alternative to traditional oatmeal that's gentle on the gut and packed with flavor.

Ingredients:

- 2 ripe plantains (yellow with black spots)
- 1 3/4 cups full-fat coconut milk
- 1/2 cup water
- 1/2 teaspoon ground cinnamon
- 1/4 teaspoon ground ginger
- Pinch of ground nutmeg
- Pinch of sea salt
- Optional toppings: berries, sliced bananas, chopped nuts (if reintroduced), coconut flakes, honey or maple syrup (to taste)

Instructions:

1. Peel the plantains and chop them into small pieces.
2. In a medium saucepan, combine the chopped plantains, coconut milk, and water.
3. Bring the mixture to a simmer over medium heat.
4. Reduce the heat to low and cook for 10-15 minutes, or until the plantains are soft and the mixture has thickened, stirring occasionally.
5. Stir in the cinnamon, ginger, nutmeg, and salt.
6. Remove the saucepan from the heat and let the porridge cool slightly before serving.
7. If desired, use an immersion blender to create a smoother consistency.
8. Divide the porridge into bowls and top with your favorite AIP-compliant toppings.

Tips:

- For a richer flavor, use canned coconut cream instead of coconut milk.
- If you prefer a thinner porridge, add more water or coconut milk.
- Feel free to experiment with different spices, such as cardamom, cloves, or allspice.
- Leftover porridge can be stored in the refrigerator for up to 3 days.

I first discovered plantain porridge when I was traveling in Central America, and I instantly fell in love with its creamy texture and comforting warmth. Now, it's a staple in my AIP breakfast rotation, and I love experimenting with different toppings to keep things interesting.

Enjoy this delicious and nourishing Plantain Porridge, a simple yet satisfying way to fuel your body and embrace the AIP lifestyle.

"Good food is like fuel for the body. It nourishes us, energizes us, and helps us to thrive."
– Unknown

Green Dream AIP Smoothie: A Vibrant Start to Your Day

Prep Time: 5 minutes **Yields:** 2 servings

This refreshing and vibrant smoothie is a powerhouse of nutrients, making it a perfect breakfast or snack option for those following the AIP diet. Packed with leafy greens, fruit, healthy fats from avocado, and creamy coconut milk, it's a delicious way to nourish your body and fuel your day.

Ingredients:

- 1 cup full-fat coconut milk (from a can or carton)
- 1/2 cup water or additional coconut milk for desired consistency
- 2 cups leafy greens (spinach, kale, or romaine lettuce)
- 1 ripe banana, frozen
- 1/2 avocado, pitted and peeled
- 1/2 cup frozen berries (strawberries, blueberries, raspberries)
- Optional add-ins:
    - 1 tablespoon collagen peptides for added protein
    - 1/2 inch piece of fresh ginger for a zingy flavor
    - 1/2 teaspoon ground cinnamon for warmth
    - Pinch of sea salt to enhance flavors

Instructions:

1. Add all ingredients to a blender.
2. Blend on high speed until smooth and creamy.
3. If the smoothie is too thick, add a bit more water or coconut milk until desired consistency is reached.
4. Taste and adjust sweetness or flavors as needed.
5. Pour into glasses and enjoy immediately!

Tips:

- For a colder smoothie, use frozen greens and/or add a few ice cubes.
- Feel free to experiment with different leafy greens and fruits based on your preferences and what's in season.
- If you don't have frozen bananas, use fresh ones and add a few ice cubes to the blender.
- Leftover smoothie can be stored in the refrigerator for up to 24 hours.

I used to dread drinking green smoothies, but this AIP version has completely changed my mind! It's so creamy and flavorful that I actually look forward to it every morning. It's become my go-to breakfast when I'm short on time or need a quick energy boost.

Indulge in this Green Dream AIP Smoothie and experience the vibrant energy it brings to your day. Cheers to your health!

"Eating healthy food fills your body with energy and nutrients. Imagine your cells smiling back at you and saying: 'Thank you!'" – Karen Salmansohn

Salmon Cakes with Avocado Salsa: A Fiesta of Flavor

Prep Time: 15 minutes **Cook Time:** 20 minutes **Yields:** 4 servings

These vibrant salmon cakes are bursting with flavor and make a satisfying AIP-compliant meal. The tender, savory salmon patties are complemented perfectly by the cool and refreshing avocado salsa, creating a symphony of textures and tastes.

Ingredients:

For the Salmon Cakes:

- 1 (14-ounce) can wild-caught salmon, drained and flaked
- 1/2 cup mashed sweet potato
- 1/4 cup chopped green onions
- 1/4 cup chopped fresh cilantro
- 1 tablespoon lemon juice
- 1 teaspoon garlic powder
- 1/2 teaspoon sea salt
- 1/4 teaspoon black pepper
- 1/4 cup cassava flour (or arrowroot flour)
- Avocado oil or ghee, for cooking

For the Avocado Salsa:

- 1 ripe avocado, diced
- 1/4 cup diced red onion
- 1/4 cup diced tomato
- 1/4 cup chopped fresh cilantro
- 1 tablespoon lime juice
- 1/2 teaspoon sea salt
- 1/4 teaspoon black pepper

Instructions:

1. In a large bowl, combine the flaked salmon, mashed sweet potato, green onions, cilantro, lemon juice, garlic powder, salt, and pepper.
2. Mix in the cassava flour until the mixture is well combined and holds its shape.
3. Form the mixture into 8 patties.
4. Heat avocado oil or ghee in a large skillet over medium heat.
5. Cook the salmon cakes for 3-4 minutes per side, or until golden brown and cooked through.
6. While the salmon cakes are cooking, prepare the avocado salsa by combining all the ingredients in a bowl.
7. Serve the salmon cakes warm, topped with the avocado salsa.

Tips:

- For extra crispiness, you can add a few tablespoons of almond flour to the salmon cake mixture.
- Feel free to adjust the amount of spice in the salsa to your liking.

- For a heartier meal, serve the salmon cakes with a side of roasted vegetables or cauliflower rice.

I remember the first time I tried salmon cakes with avocado salsa. I was skeptical at first, but the combination of flavors and textures was so delicious and satisfying that it quickly became one of my favorite AIP meals. It's a perfect example of how vibrant and flavorful AIP cooking can be.

Enjoy these flavorful Salmon Cakes with Avocado Salsa as a delicious and nutritious meal that's perfect for any occasion!

"Cooking is like love. It should be entered into with abandon or not at all." – Harriet Van Horne

Zucchini Fritters: Crispy Golden Bites of summer

Prep Time: 10 minutes **Cook Time:** 15 minutes **Yields:** 10-12 fritters

These crispy and flavorful zucchini fritters are a delightful way to enjoy this abundant summer squash while adhering to the AIP diet. They're simple to make, packed with nutrients, and a delicious addition to any meal.

Ingredients:

- 2 medium zucchini, grated (about 2 cups)
- 1/2 medium yellow onion, finely chopped
- 2 cloves garlic, minced
- 1/2 cup chopped fresh herbs (parsley, dill, mint, or a combination)
- 1/4 cup cassava flour (or arrowroot flour)
- 1 large egg
- 1/2 teaspoon sea salt
- 1/4 teaspoon black pepper
- Avocado oil or ghee, for frying

Instructions:

1. Place the grated zucchini in a colander set over a bowl. Sprinkle with salt and let sit for 10 minutes to release excess moisture.
2. Press the zucchini firmly to squeeze out any remaining liquid.
3. In a large bowl, combine the zucchini, onion, garlic, herbs, cassava flour, egg, salt, and pepper. Mix well until a batter forms.
4. Heat avocado oil or ghee in a large skillet over medium heat.
5. Drop spoonfuls of the batter into the hot oil, forming small fritters.
6. Cook for 2-3 minutes per side, or until golden brown and crispy.
7. Transfer the fritters to a paper towel-lined plate to drain excess oil.
8. Serve warm with your favorite AIP-compliant dipping sauce, such as avocado mayo or chimichurri sauce.

Tips:

- If the batter is too wet, add a bit more cassava flour to achieve a thicker consistency.
- For a crispier fritter, don't overcrowd the pan. Cook in batches if needed
- You can experiment with different herbs and spices to create your own unique flavor combinations.

I remember growing up with an abundance of zucchini from my grandmother's garden. She would always make these delicious zucchini fritters, and I loved helping her grate the zucchini and mix the batter. It's a simple recipe that brings back fond memories of summer days spent in the kitchen with my family.

Chicken Apple Sausage Hash: Hearty & Wholesome

Prep Time: 10 minutes **Cook Time:** 20 minutes **Yields:** 4 servings

This savory hash is a delicious and satisfying way to start your day on the AIP diet. The combination of chicken apple sausage, sweet potatoes, onions, and warming spices creates a hearty and flavorful breakfast that will keep you feeling full and energized.

Ingredients:

- 1 pound AIP-compliant chicken apple sausage, casings removed and crumbled
- 2 medium sweet potatoes, peeled and diced
- 1 medium yellow onion, diced
- 1 tablespoon avocado oil or ghee
- 1/2 teaspoon dried sage
- 1/4 teaspoon dried thyme
- 1/4 teaspoon salt
- 1/4 teaspoon black pepper
- Fresh chopped parsley, for garnish (optional)

Instructions:

1. Heat the avocado oil or ghee in a large skillet over medium heat.
2. Add the crumbled sausage and cook until browned, breaking it up with a spatula as it cooks.
3. Add the diced sweet potatoes and onions to the skillet. Cook for 10-15 minutes, stirring occasionally, until the sweet potatoes are tender and slightly browned.
4. Stir in the sage, thyme, salt, and pepper. Cook for an additional minute to combine the flavors.
5. Serve warm, garnished with fresh parsley if desired.

I love this hash because it's so versatile. I often add different vegetables depending on what I have on hand, such as diced carrots, chopped kale, or even shredded Brussels sprouts. It's a great way to use up leftovers and create a unique and flavorful breakfast every time.

"A healthy outside starts from the inside." – Robert Urich

AIP Breakfast Bowl: Nourishing & Vibrant

Prep Time: 10 minutes **Cook Time:** 15 minutes **Yields:** 2 servings

This colorful and nutrient-rich breakfast bowl is a delicious and satisfying way to start your day on the AIP diet. The creamy mashed sweet potato base is topped with sautéed greens, avocado slices, and a perfectly poached egg for a balanced and flavorful meal.

Ingredients:

- 2 medium sweet potatoes, peeled and cubed
- 1 tablespoon ghee or avocado oil
- 1/4 cup full-fat coconut milk (or more, as needed for desired consistency)
- 1/4 teaspoon sea salt
- 4 cups chopped leafy greens (kale, spinach, or collard greens)
- 1/2 avocado, sliced
- 2 large eggs
- 1 tablespoon apple cider vinegar

Instructions:

1. Place the sweet potatoes in a pot and cover with water. Bring to a boil, then reduce heat and simmer until tender (about 15 minutes).
2. Drain the sweet potatoes and return them to the pot. Mash them with ghee, coconut milk, and salt until smooth and creamy.
3. While the sweet potatoes are cooking, heat a skillet over medium heat. Add the leafy greens and sauté until wilted, about 3-5 minutes.
4. To poach the eggs, fill a small saucepan with 2-3 inches of water and bring to a simmer. Add the apple cider vinegar. Crack each egg into a small bowl, then gently slide them into the simmering water. Cook for 3-4 minutes, or until the whites are set and the yolks are still runny. Remove the eggs with a slotted spoon and drain on a paper towel-lined plate.
5. Divide the mashed sweet potatoes between two bowls. Top with sautéed greens, avocado slices, and a poached egg. Season with additional salt and pepper, if desired.

Enjoy this nourishing and flavorful AIP Breakfast Bowl as a delicious and satisfying way to fuel your body and start your day right.

"Healthy eating is a journey, not a destination. It's about finding what works for you and making sustainable changes that you can stick with for the long haul." - Unknown

AIP Banana Bread: A Sweet and Satisfying Treat

Prep Time: 15 minutes **Cook Time:** 45-55 minutes **Yields:** 1 loaf

This moist and flavorful banana bread is a delightful AIP-compliant treat that satisfies your sweet cravings without compromising your health goals. Made with simple, wholesome ingredients like almond flour, coconut sugar, and ripe bananas, it's a delicious way to enjoy a classic comfort food while nourishing your body.

Ingredients:

- 3 ripe bananas, mashed
- 1/3 cup coconut oil, melted and cooled
- 1/4 cup honey or maple syrup
- 2 large eggs
- 1 teaspoon vanilla extract
- 2 cups almond flour
- 1/4 cup tapioca flour (or arrowroot flour)
- 1 teaspoon baking soda
- 1/2 teaspoon salt
- 1/2 cup chopped walnuts or pecans (optional)

Instructions:

1. Preheat oven to 350°F (175°C). Grease and flour a 9x5 inch loaf pan.
2. In a large bowl, whisk together the mashed bananas, melted coconut oil, honey or maple syrup, eggs, and vanilla extract.
3. In a separate bowl, combine the almond flour, tapioca flour, baking soda, and salt.
4. Add the dry ingredients to the wet ingredients and mix until just combined. Do not overmix.
5. Fold in the chopped nuts, if using.
6. Pour the batter into the prepared loaf pan.
7. Bake for 45-55 minutes, or until a toothpick inserted into the center comes out clean.
8. Let the bread cool in the pan for 10 minutes before transferring to a wire rack to cool completely.

Tips:

- For a more intense banana flavor, use overripe bananas with brown spots.
- If you don't have tapioca flour, you can substitute arrowroot flour.
- Feel free to add other AIP-compliant mix-ins, such as shredded

- coconut, chopped dates, or dried cranberries.
- Store the banana bread in an airtight container at room temperature for up to 3 days or in the refrigerator for up to 5 days.

I used to think banana bread was off-limits on the AIP diet, but this recipe proved me wrong! It's so moist, flavorful, and satisfying that it's become a staple in my house. I love that it's made with simple, wholesome ingredients that I feel good about feeding my family.

Indulge in this delicious AIP Banana Bread, knowing that you're nourishing your body with wholesome ingredients and satisfying your sweet tooth without compromising your health goals.

Lunch

"Healthy eating is not about deprivation; it's about nourishment." - Unknown

Turkey Lettuce Wraps: A Flavorful & Fun AIP Meal

Prep Time: 15 minutes **Cook Time:** 15 minutes **Yields:** 4 servings

These versatile and satisfying lettuce wraps are a fantastic way to enjoy a light yet protein-packed meal on the AIP diet. The seasoned ground turkey filling is bursting with flavor, while the crisp lettuce leaves provide a refreshing crunch. The best part? You can customize them with your favorite AIP-compliant toppings to create endless variations.

Ingredients:

- 1 pound ground turkey
- 1 tablespoon avocado oil or ghee
- 1/2 medium yellow onion, diced
- 2 cloves garlic, minced
- 1/2 cup chopped carrots
- 1/2 cup chopped celery
- 1/2 teaspoon ground ginger
- 1/4 teaspoon sea salt
- 1/4 teaspoon black pepper
- 1 head butter lettuce, leaves separated
- Optional toppings:
    - Avocado slices
    - Shredded carrots
    - Chopped cucumbers
    - Sliced green onions
    - Chopped cilantro
    - AIP-compliant mayonnaise or dressing

Instructions:

1. Heat the avocado oil or ghee in a large skillet over medium heat.
2. Add the ground turkey and cook until browned, breaking it up with a spatula as it cooks.
3. Add the diced onion, garlic, carrots, and celery to the skillet. Cook for 5-7 minutes, or until the vegetables are softened.
4. Stir in the ginger, salt, and pepper. Cook for an additional minute to combine the flavors.
5. To assemble the wraps, place a lettuce leaf on a plate and spoon a generous amount of the turkey mixture into the center.
6. Top with your favorite AIP-compliant toppings and enjoy!

Tips:

- For extra flavor, add chopped mushrooms, shredded cabbage, or

- diced water chestnuts (if tolerated) to the turkey mixture.
- Feel free to experiment with different herbs and spices to customize the flavor profile of the filling.
- If you prefer a warmer wrap, briefly heat the lettuce leaves in a dry skillet or microwave before filling.

I love these lettuce wraps because they're so customizable. I can change up the toppings depending on what I have in the fridge or what I'm in the mood for. Sometimes I go for a classic Asian-inspired flavor profile with avocado, carrots, and cilantro. Other times, I'll add a Mexican twist with salsa, guacamole, and jalapenos.

Embrace the versatility of these Turkey Lettuce Wraps and have fun creating your own delicious and nutritious combinations!

"Soup is a lot like a hug in a bowl." – Unknown

Carrot Ginger Soup: A Warming Embrace in a Bowl

Prep Time: 10 minutes **Cook Time:** 30 minutes **Yields:** 4 servings

This velvety smooth and fragrant soup is a comforting classic on the AIP diet. The sweetness of the carrots beautifully balances the warm spice of ginger, while the coconut milk adds a creamy richness. It's a nourishing and flavorful meal that's perfect for chilly days or when you're feeling under the weather.

Ingredients:

- 2 tablespoons avocado oil or ghee
- 1 large yellow onion, diced
- 2 cloves garlic, minced
- 1 tablespoon freshly grated ginger (or 1 teaspoon dried ginger)
- 1 1/2 pounds carrots, peeled and chopped
- 4 cups vegetable broth
- 1 cup full-fat coconut milk (or more, to taste)
- 1/2 teaspoon sea salt
- 1/4 teaspoon black pepper
- Optional garnishes: fresh cilantro, lime wedges, a drizzle of olive oil

Instructions:

1. Heat the avocado oil or ghee in a large pot or Dutch oven over medium heat.
2. Add the diced onion and cook until softened and translucent, about 5 minutes.
3. Add the minced garlic and grated ginger and cook for an additional minute, until fragrant.
4. Add the chopped carrots and vegetable broth to the pot. Bring to a boil, then reduce heat and simmer until the carrots are tender, about 20 minutes.
5. Remove the pot from the heat and carefully transfer the soup to a blender. Blend until smooth and creamy. (Alternatively, you can use an immersion blender directly in the pot.)
6. Return the soup to the pot and stir in the coconut milk, salt, and pepper. Heat gently over low heat, stirring occasionally, until warmed through.
7. Serve warm, garnished with fresh cilantro, a squeeze of lime, and a drizzle of olive oil, if desired.

Tips:

- For a richer flavor, use homemade bone broth instead of vegetable broth.
- If you don't have fresh ginger, you can use dried ginger powder, but

- use a smaller amount as it's more potent.
- Feel free to adjust the amount of coconut milk to achieve your desired consistency.
- Leftover soup can be stored in the refrigerator for up to 5 days or frozen for later.

I discovered this soup when I first started the AIP diet, and it quickly became a staple in my meal rotation. It's so simple to make, yet incredibly satisfying and nourishing. The warm flavors of ginger and the creamy coconut milk always make me feel comforted and grounded.

Embrace the warmth and comfort of this delicious Carrot Ginger Soup as a nourishing addition to your AIP journey.

"Healthy food is the most delicious medicine." - Unknown

Chicken Salad with Avocado Mayo: A Creamy & Refreshing AIP Lunch

Prep Time: 10 minutes **Yields:** 4 servings

This creamy and refreshing chicken salad is a delicious and nutritious lunch option on the AIP diet. Made with shredded chicken, homemade avocado mayo, crunchy celery, and sweet grapes, it's a flavorful and satisfying meal that's perfect for meal prep or a quick lunch on the go.

Ingredients:

- 2 cups cooked, shredded chicken (from a rotisserie chicken or leftover roast)
- 1/2 cup celery, finely chopped
- 1/2 cup red grapes, halved
- 1/4 cup chopped fresh parsley or dill
- Salt and pepper to taste

For the Avocado Mayo:

- 1 ripe avocado, pitted and peeled
- 2 tablespoons lemon juice
- 2 tablespoons olive oil
- 1/4 teaspoon garlic powder
- 1/4 teaspoon onion powder
- 1/4 teaspoon salt
- 1/4 teaspoon black pepper

Instructions:

1. In a food processor or blender, combine all the avocado mayo ingredients and blend until smooth and creamy.
2. If the mixture is too thick, add a tablespoon of water at a time until desired consistency is reached.
3. In a large bowl, combine the shredded chicken, chopped celery, halved grapes, and chopped parsley or dill.
4. Stir in the avocado mayo until the chicken salad is well coated.
5. Season with additional salt and pepper to taste.
6. Chill the chicken salad in the refrigerator for at least 30 minutes before serving.
7. Enjoy on its own, in lettuce wraps, or over a bed of greens.

Tips:

- For a spicier kick, add a pinch of cayenne pepper or a dash of hot sauce to the avocado mayo.
- If you don't have a food processor or blender, you can mash the avocado with a fork and whisk in the remaining ingredients.
- Feel free to add other AIP-compliant ingredients to the salad, such as chopped apples, diced cucumbers, or shredded carrots.

I've always loved chicken salad, but the traditional recipe with mayonnaise was off-limits on the AIP diet. That's when I discovered the magic of avocado mayo! It's a healthier and more flavorful alternative that makes this chicken salad even more delicious.

Indulge in this creamy and refreshing Chicken Salad with Avocado Mayo as a satisfying and nutritious AIP-compliant meal.

"A salad is not a meal. It is a style." - Fran Lebowitz

Sweet Potato & Kale Salad: A Vibrant Symphony of Fall Flavors

Prep Time: 15 minutes **Cook Time:** 30 minutes **Yields:** 4 servings

This hearty and nourishing salad is a celebration of fall flavors, perfect for enjoying on the AIP diet. The sweetness of roasted sweet potatoes, the earthy kale, the tangy cranberries, and the crunchy pecans create a delightful symphony of textures and tastes that will leave you feeling satisfied and energized.

Ingredients:

- 2 medium sweet potatoes, peeled and diced
- 1 bunch of kale, stems removed and chopped
- 1/2 cup dried cranberries
- 1/2 cup chopped pecans
- 2 tablespoons olive oil
- 1/4 teaspoon salt
- 1/4 teaspoon black pepper
- 1/4 cup apple cider vinegar
- 1 tablespoon Dijon mustard
- 1 tablespoon honey or maple syrup (optional)

Instructions:

1. Preheat the oven to 400°F (200°C).
2. Toss the diced sweet potatoes with 1 tablespoon of olive oil, salt, and pepper on a baking sheet.
3. Roast for 20-25 minutes, or until tender and slightly browned.
4. While the sweet potatoes are roasting, place the chopped kale in a large bowl.
5. Drizzle with 1 tablespoon of olive oil and massage the kale with your hands for a few minutes, until it softens and becomes tender.
6. In a small bowl, whisk together the apple cider vinegar, Dijon mustard, honey or maple syrup (if using), salt, and pepper.
7. Once the sweet potatoes are roasted, add them to the bowl with the kale.
8. Add the cranberries and pecans.
9. Drizzle the dressing over the salad and toss to coat.
10. Serve immediately or chill for later.

Tips:

- For a more robust flavor, add a pinch of smoked paprika or cumin to the sweet potatoes while roasting.
- If you prefer a sweeter salad, add more honey or maple syrup to the dressing.
- You can substitute other dried fruits, such as chopped dates or apricots, for the cranberries.

- To make the salad nut-free, omit the pecans.

I love this salad because it's so versatile and satisfying. I often make a big batch at the beginning of the week and enjoy it for lunch or dinner throughout the week. It's also a great dish to bring to potlucks or gatherings.

Embrace the vibrant flavors and textures of this delicious Sweet Potato & Kale Salad as a nourishing and satisfying addition to your AIP lifestyle.

"Waste not, want not." – Proverb

Leftover Roasted Chicken & Veggie Bowls: Flavorful Fuel in a Flash

Prep Time: 5 minutes **Yields:** 2 servings

This vibrant and satisfying bowl is a fantastic way to repurpose leftover roasted chicken and vegetables into a delicious and nutritious AIP-compliant lunch. It's a quick and easy meal that's packed with protein, fiber, and essential nutrients to keep you feeling full and energized.

Ingredients:

- 2 cups cooked, shredded chicken
- 2 cups leftover roasted vegetables (any combination of your favorites)
- 1 cup cooked cauliflower rice
- 1/4 cup chopped fresh herbs (parsley, cilantro, or basil)
- 1/4 avocado, sliced or diced
- Optional toppings:
    - AIP-compliant dressing (such as balsamic vinaigrette or lemon-herb dressing)
    - Chopped nuts or seeds (if tolerated)
    - A drizzle of olive oil

Instructions:

1. Divide the cauliflower rice between two bowls.
2. Top with the shredded chicken and roasted vegetables.
3. Add the chopped herbs and avocado slices or dices.
4. Drizzle with your favorite AIP-compliant dressing, if desired.
5. Enjoy immediately!

Tips:

- Feel free to use any leftover roasted vegetables you have on hand, such as sweet potatoes, carrots, broccoli, or Brussels sprouts.
- You can also add other AIP-compliant ingredients to your bowl, such as chopped hard-boiled eggs or leftover cooked bacon.
- If you don't have leftover roasted vegetables, you can quickly roast some fresh vegetables in the oven while the cauliflower rice is cooking.

I often roast a whole chicken on the weekends, and I love using the leftovers to create these delicious and nutritious bowls throughout the week. It's a great way to save time and money while still enjoying a satisfying and healthy meal.

Transform your leftovers into a culinary masterpiece with these flavorful and easy Leftover Roasted Chicken & Veggie Bowls!

AIP Zucchini Noodles with Nomato Sauce: A Flavorful & Comforting Dish

Prep Time: 15 minutes **Cook Time:** 45 minutes **Yields:** 4 servings

This hearty and flavorful dish is a perfect alternative to traditional pasta for those starting their AIP journey. Spiralized zucchini noodles, or "zoodles," are tossed in a rich and savory "nomato" (no tomato) sauce made with wholesome, AIP-compliant ingredients. It's a satisfying and nutritious meal that's surprisingly easy to prepare and surprisingly close to the real thing!

Ingredients:

For the Nomato Sauce:

- 1 pound ground beef or lamb
- 1 medium onion, diced
- 2 cloves garlic, minced
- 1 tablespoon avocado oil or ghee
- 2 cups peeled and diced carrots
- 1 medium beet, peeled and diced
- 1/2 cup chopped celery
- 1/2 cup chopped parsnips
- 1/2 teaspoon dried oregano
- 1/2 teaspoon dried basil
- 1/4 teaspoon sea salt
- 1/4 teaspoon black pepper
- 1 bay leaf
- 4 cups bone broth (or vegetable broth)
- 1 tablespoon lemon juice

For the Zucchini Noodles:

- 4 medium zucchini, spiralized or julienned into noodle shapes

Instructions:

1. Heat the avocado oil or ghee in a large pot or Dutch oven over medium heat.
2. Add the ground beef or lamb and cook until browned, breaking it up with a spatula as it cooks.
3. Add the diced onion and minced garlic to the pot.
4. Cook for 5-7 minutes, or until the onion is softened and translucent.
5. Stir in the diced carrots, beets, celery, parsnips, oregano, basil, salt, pepper, and bay leaf.
6. Cook for an additional 5 minutes, stirring occasionally.
7. Pour in the bone broth (or vegetable broth) and lemon juice. Bring to a boil, then reduce heat and simmer for 30 minutes, or until the vegetables are tender and the sauce has thickened.
8. Taste and adjust seasoning as needed. Remove the bay leaf before serving.
9. While the sauce is simmering, spiralize or julienne the zucchini into noodle shapes.
10. Once the sauce is ready, add the zucchini noodles to the pot and toss gently to coat.

11. Cook for 1-2 minutes, or until the noodles are heated through but still slightly firm.
12. Serve immediately, topped with fresh basil or parsley, if desired.

Tips for Beginners:

- Beets and carrots provide the rich, earthy flavor and color that mimics tomatoes in this AIP-friendly sauce.
- You can adjust the amount of vegetables to your preference.
- For a smoother sauce, use an immersion blender or carefully transfer the sauce to a blender and puree until smooth before returning to the pot.

When I first started AIP, I missed my favorite pasta dishes. This recipe was a game-changer! The combination of flavors in the "nomato" sauce is so rich and satisfying, and the zucchini noodles provide the perfect texture. It's a dish that my whole family enjoys, even those who aren't following AIP.

"Chicken soup is good for the soul." – Jewish Proverb

Nourishing Chicken Soup: Your AIP Comfort in a Bowl

Prep Time: 15 minutes **Cook Time:** 45 minutes **Yields:** 6 servings

This comforting and flavorful chicken soup is a staple for anyone following the AIP diet. It's packed with nourishing vegetables and tender chicken, making it a delicious and healing meal that's perfect for chilly days or when you're feeling under the weather.

Ingredients:

- 1 whole chicken (about 3 pounds), cut into pieces, or 2 pounds boneless, skinless chicken thighs or breasts
- 8 cups bone broth (homemade or store-bought)
- 2 carrots, peeled and chopped
- 2 stalks celery, chopped
- 1 medium yellow onion, diced
- 2 cloves garlic, minced
- 1-inch piece of fresh ginger, grated
- 1 teaspoon dried thyme
- 1/2 teaspoon dried rosemary
- 1/4 teaspoon sea salt
- 1/4 teaspoon black pepper
- Optional add-ins:
    - 1/2 cup chopped parsnips
    - 1/2 cup chopped turnips
    - 1/2 cup chopped kale or spinach
    - 1/4 cup chopped fresh parsley, for garnish

Instructions:

1. In a large pot or Dutch oven, combine the chicken pieces and bone broth.
2. Bring to a boil, then reduce heat and simmer for 30 minutes, or until the chicken is cooked through.
3. Carefully remove the chicken from the pot and set it aside to cool slightly.
4. Add the carrots, celery, onion, garlic, and ginger to the pot.
5. Bring to a simmer and cook for 10-15 minutes, or until the vegetables are tender.
6. Once the chicken is cool enough to handle, remove the skin and bones (if using a whole chicken) and shred the meat with two forks.
7. Return the shredded chicken to the pot along with the thyme, rosemary, salt, and pepper.
8. Stir to combine.
9. If desired, add the parsnips, turnips, kale, or spinach to the pot and cook until tender.
10. Let the soup simmer for an additional 5-10 minutes to allow the flavors to meld.
11. Ladle into bowls and garnish with fresh parsley, if desired.

Tips:

- For a richer flavor, use homemade bone broth made from chicken bones or beef bones.
- Feel free to adjust the amount of vegetables to your preference.
- If you don't have fresh herbs, you can use dried herbs.
- Leftover soup can be stored in the refrigerator for up to 5 days or frozen for later.

Growing up, my mom's chicken soup was my ultimate comfort food. Whenever I was feeling sick or down, a warm bowl of her soup always made me feel better. Now, I make my own AIP version, and it's just as comforting and nourishing.

Enjoy this classic and nourishing Chicken Soup as a delicious and healing meal on the AIP diet.

> "Eating healthy food fills your body with energy and nutrients. Imagine your cells smiling back at you and saying: 'Thank you!'" – Karen Salmansohn

Avocado Tuna Salad: A Creamy & Flavorful AIP Delight

Prep Time: 10 minutes **Yields:** 4 servings

This creamy and flavorful tuna salad is a healthy and delicious alternative to the traditional mayonnaise-based version, perfect for those following the AIP diet. The avocado adds a rich and creamy texture, while the lemon juice and herbs provide a bright and refreshing flavor. It's a versatile dish that can be enjoyed on its own, in lettuce wraps, or as a filling for stuffed vegetables.

Ingredients:

- 2 (5-ounce) cans tuna, drained (preferably packed in olive oil)
- 1 ripe avocado, pitted and mashed
- 1/4 cup diced celery
- 1/4 cup diced red onion
- 1 tablespoon lemon juice
- 1 tablespoon chopped fresh parsley
- 1/2 teaspoon sea salt
- 1/4 teaspoon black pepper
- Optional add-ins:
  - 1/4 cup chopped fresh dill
  - 1/4 teaspoon Dijon mustard (AIP-compliant, no added sugar)
  - A pinch of cayenne pepper or red pepper flakes (if you like a little spice)

Instructions:

1. In a medium bowl, combine the drained tuna, mashed avocado, celery, red onion, lemon juice, parsley, salt, and pepper.
2. Mix well until all ingredients are evenly combined.
3. Taste and adjust seasoning as needed. Add any optional ingredients and mix again.
4. Serve immediately or chill in the refrigerator for later.

Tips:

- For a smoother texture, you can use a food processor to combine the ingredients.
- If you don't have fresh herbs, you can use dried herbs, but use half the amount as they are more concentrated.
- Feel free to experiment with different herbs and spices to customize the flavor profile.
- Leftover tuna salad can be stored in an airtight container in the refrigerator for up to 3 days.

I used to love tuna salad sandwiches, but mayonnaise was a no-go on AIP. This recipe was a lifesaver! The avocado adds such a creamy and luxurious texture, and the lemon juice and herbs give it a bright and fresh flavor. It's become a staple in my lunch rotation.

Enjoy this delicious and nutritious Avocado Tuna Salad as a healthy and satisfying meal on the AIP diet!

Cauliflower Rice Stir-Fry: A Rainbow of Flavors & Textures (AIP-Friendly)

Prep Time: 15 minutes **Cook Time:** 20 minutes **Yields:** 4 servings

This vibrant and flavorful stir-fry is a quick and easy way to enjoy a healthy and satisfying meal, whether you're in the elimination or reintroduction phase of the AIP diet. The cauliflower rice provides a light and fluffy base, while the colorful vegetables and your choice of protein add a burst of nutrients and flavor.

Ingredients:

- 1 head of cauliflower, riced (about 4 cups)
- 1 tablespoon avocado oil or ghee
- 1/2 medium yellow onion, diced
- 2 cloves garlic, minced
- 1 cup broccoli florets
- 1 cup sliced mushrooms
- 1/2 cup chopped carrots
- 1/4 cup chopped green onions
- 1/4 cup chopped fresh cilantro
- 1-inch piece of fresh ginger, grated or minced
- 2 tablespoons coconut aminos
- 1 tablespoon lime juice
- 1/2 teaspoon sea salt
- 1/4 teaspoon black pepper
- Your choice of protein:
  - 1 pound cooked, shredded chicken
  - 1 pound cooked ground beef or pork
  - 1 pound cooked shrimp

Optional Add-ins:

- **Reintroduction Phase:** 1 red bell pepper, diced & 1 green bell pepper, diced
- **Elimination Phase:** 1/2 cup chopped zucchini & 1/2 cup chopped butternut squash

Instructions:

1. If using a whole head of cauliflower, remove the leaves and core, then grate or pulse the florets in a food processor until they resemble rice grains.
2. Heat the avocado oil or ghee in a large skillet or wok over medium-high heat. Add the diced onion and cook until softened, about 3 minutes. Add the minced garlic, broccoli florets, mushrooms, and carrots. Cook for 5-7 minutes, or until the vegetables are tender-crisp.
3. If you're in the elimination phase, add the chopped zucchini and butternut squash to the skillet and cook until tender, about 5 minutes.
4. If you're in the reintroduction phase and tolerating nightshades, add the diced bell peppers to the skillet and cook until tender-crisp, about 5 minutes.

5. Add the riced cauliflower, green onions, cilantro, ginger, coconut aminos, lime juice, salt, and pepper to the skillet. Stir-fry for 5-7 minutes, or until the cauliflower rice is heated through and tender.
6. in your choice of cooked protein and cook until heated through.
7. Serve immediately, garnished with additional cilantro, if desired.

Tips:

- For a spicier stir-fry, add a pinch of red pepper flakes or a dash of hot sauce.
- Feel free to substitute other AIP-compliant vegetables in either phase.
- You can use pre-made cauliflower rice to save time.

I love making this stir-fry because it's adaptable to different phases of AIP. During the elimination phase, I use zucchini and butternut squash for color and variety. Once I reintroduced bell peppers, I enjoyed the extra sweetness and crunch they added!

"Healthy eating is not about deprivation; it's about nourishment." – Unknown

Salmon Salad with Lemon-Dill Dressing: A Light & Zesty AIP Meal

Prep Time: 10 minutes **Cook Time:** 15-20 minutes (for cooking salmon) **Yields:** 4 servings

This refreshing and flavorful salmon salad is a nutritious and satisfying meal for those following the AIP diet. The flaky salmon is perfectly complemented by the zesty lemon-dill dressing, while the addition of crunchy vegetables adds texture and variety. It's a versatile dish that can be enjoyed on its own, in lettuce cups, or atop a bed of greens.

Ingredients:

- 1 pound salmon fillet, skin removed (wild-caught is best)
- 1/2 cup diced celery
- 1/4 cup diced red onion
- 1/4 cup chopped fresh dill
- Salt and pepper to taste

For the Lemon-Dill Dressing:

- 1/4 cup extra virgin olive oil
- 2 tablespoons lemon juice
- 1 tablespoon chopped fresh dill
- 1/2 teaspoon garlic powder
- 1/4 teaspoon onion powder
- 1/4 teaspoon sea salt
- 1/4 teaspoon black pepper

Instructions:

1. Preheat oven to 400°F (200°C). Place the salmon fillet on a baking sheet lined with parchment paper.
2. Season with salt and pepper. Bake for 15-20 minutes, or until cooked through and flaky.
3. While the salmon is baking, whisk together all the dressing ingredients in a small bowl until well combined.
4. Once the salmon is cooked, let it cool slightly. Then, use a fork to flake it into bite-sized pieces.
5. In a large bowl, combine the flaked salmon, diced celery, red onion, and chopped dill.
6. Pour the lemon-dill dressing over the salmon mixture and toss gently to combine.
7. Serve the salad immediately or chill in the refrigerator for later.
8. Enjoy on its own, in lettuce wraps, or over a bed of greens.

Tips:

- For a richer flavor, use homemade mayonnaise (AIP-compliant) instead of olive oil in the dressing.
- Feel free to add other AIP-compliant vegetables to the salad, such as diced cucumbers, chopped radishes, or shredded carrots.

- If you don't have fresh dill, you can use dried dill, but use half the amount as it's more concentrated.

I love this salmon salad because it's so light and refreshing, yet still incredibly satisfying. It's my go-to lunch on hot summer days, and the leftovers are perfect for a quick and easy dinner.

Indulge in this delicious and nutritious Salmon Salad with Lemon-Dill Dressing as a light and flavorful meal on the AIP diet!

"Healthy eating is not about deprivation; it's about nourishment." – Unknown

Dinner

Lemon Herb Baked Chicken: A Simple & Flavorful AIP Staple

Prep Time: 10 minutes **Cook Time:** 25-30 minutes **Yields:** 4 servings

This juicy and flavorful baked chicken is a staple in any AIP kitchen. The combination of bright lemon zest and juice, aromatic herbs, and garlic creates a simple yet satisfying dish that's perfect for weeknight dinners or meal prepping.

Ingredients:

- 4 boneless, skinless chicken breasts (organic, free-range if possible)
- 2 tablespoons olive oil* 1 lemon, zested and juiced
- 2 cloves garlic, minced
- 1 teaspoon dried oregano
- 1/2 teaspoon dried thyme
- 1/4 teaspoon sea salt
- 1/4 teaspoon black pepper
- Fresh chopped parsley, for garnish

Instructions:

1. Preheat your oven to 400°F (200°C).
2. Pat the chicken breasts dry with paper towels.
3. Place them in a baking dish.
4. In a small bowl, whisk together the olive oil, lemon zest, lemon juice, minced garlic, oregano, thyme, salt, and pepper.
5. Pour the marinade over the chicken breasts, turning them to coat evenly.
6. Let them marinate for at least 15 minutes, or up to an hour.
7. Bake the chicken for 25-30 minutes, or until cooked through (internal temperature should reach 165°F or 74°C).
8. Garnish with fresh chopped parsley and serve with your favorite AIP-compliant side dishes, such as roasted vegetables or cauliflower rice.

Tips:

- For extra flavor, add a pinch of red pepper flakes or a dash of hot sauce to the marinade.
- If you have time, marinate the chicken overnight for even more intense flavor.
- To prevent the chicken from drying out, baste it with the pan juices a few times during baking.

- Leftover chicken can be used in salads, soups, or wraps.

I love this recipe because it's so easy to make and always turns out perfectly juicy and flavorful. It's a great dish to have in your back pocket for busy weeknights when you don't have a lot of time to cook.

Enjoy this simple and delicious Lemon Herb Baked Chicken as a healthy and satisfying meal on the AIP diet!

"Healthy food is the most delicious medicine." - Unknown

AIP Shepherd's Pie: Comfort Food with a Healing Twist

Prep Time: 20 minutes **Cook Time:** 45 minutes **Yields:** 6 servings

This comforting and flavorful Shepherd's Pie is a hearty and satisfying meal that's perfect for the AIP diet. Made with nutrient-dense ingredients like ground lamb (or beef), sweet potatoes, and a medley of vegetables, it's a delicious way to nourish your body while enjoying a classic comfort food.

Ingredients:

- Meat Filling:
    - 1 pound ground lamb (or beef)
    - 1 tablespoon avocado oil or ghee
    - 1 medium onion, diced
    - 2 cloves garlic, minced
    - 2 carrots, peeled and chopped
    - 2 stalks celery, chopped
    - 1 cup chopped mushrooms
    - 1/2 teaspoon dried thyme
    - 1/2 teaspoon dried rosemary
    - 1/4 teaspoon sea salt
    - 1/4 teaspoon black pepper
    - 1 cup bone broth
- Sweet Potato Mash:
    - 2 pounds sweet potatoes, peeled and cubed
    - 1/4 cup full-fat coconut milk (or more, for desired consistency)
    - 2 tablespoons ghee or avocado oil
    - 1/4 teaspoon sea salt
    - 1/4 teaspoon black pepper

Instructions:

1. Place the cubed sweet potatoes in a pot and cover with water. Bring to a boil, then reduce heat and simmer until tender (about 15 minutes).
2. Drain and mash with coconut milk, ghee, salt, and pepper until smooth and creamy.
3. While the sweet potatoes are cooking, heat the avocado oil or ghee in a large skillet over medium heat.
4. Add the ground lamb (or beef) and cook until browned, breaking it up with a spatula as it cooks.
5. Add the diced onion, minced garlic, chopped carrots, celery, and mushrooms to the skillet.
6. Cook for 5-7 minutes, or until the vegetables are softened.
7. Stir in the thyme, rosemary, salt, and pepper. Cook for an additional minute to combine the flavors.
8. Pour in the bone broth and bring to a simmer. Cook for 10-15 minutes, or until the sauce has thickened slightly.

9. Preheat oven to 375°F (190°C). Spread the meat filling evenly in a baking dish.
10. Top with the mashed sweet potatoes, smoothing it out with a spatula.
11. Bake for 20-25 minutes, or until the sweet potatoes are golden brown and the filling is bubbly.
12. Let cool slightly before serving.
13. Enjoy as a comforting and nutritious meal on the AIP diet.

Tips:

- For a richer flavor, use homemade bone broth instead of store-bought.
- Feel free to add other AIP-compliant vegetables to the filling, such as chopped broccoli or cauliflower florets.
- If you don't have fresh herbs, you can use dried herbs, but use half the amount as they are more concentrated.
- Leftover Shepherd's Pie can be stored in the refrigerator for up to 4 days or frozen for later.

I used to love Shepherd's Pie growing up, but the traditional recipe with potatoes and dairy was off-limits on the AIP diet. This recipe has become my go-to comfort food on chilly evenings. The sweet potatoes are so creamy and flavorful, and the meat filling is hearty and satisfying.

Indulge in this comforting and delicious AIP Shepherd's Pie as a nourishing and satisfying meal that's good for your body and soul.

"Eating healthy should be a joy, not a chore." – Unknown

Baked Salmon with Roasted Vegetables: A Nourishing Symphony of Flavors

Prep Time: 15 minutes **Cook Time:** 25-30 minutes **Yields:** 4 servings

This simple yet elegant dish is a perfect example of how delicious and satisfying AIP meals can be. The tender, flaky salmon is complemented by a medley of colorful roasted vegetables, creating a symphony of flavors and textures that nourish the body and delight the taste buds.

Ingredients:

- 4 (6-ounce) salmon fillets, skin-on (wild-caught is best)
- Assorted AIP-compliant vegetables, such as:
    - 1 head broccoli, cut into florets
    - 2 cups Brussels sprouts, halved
    - 1 sweet potato, peeled and cubed
    - 1 red onion, cut into wedges
- 2 tablespoons avocado oil or ghee
- 1 lemon, zested and juiced
- 2 cloves garlic, minced
- 1 teaspoon dried oregano
- 1/2 teaspoon dried thyme
- 1/4 teaspoon sea salt
- 1/4 teaspoon black pepper
- Fresh chopped parsley, for garnish

Instructions:

1. Preheat your oven to 400°F (200°C).
2. In a large bowl, toss the vegetables with avocado oil or ghee, salt, and pepper.
3. Spread them out on a baking sheet in a single layer.
4. Roast the vegetables for 15-20 minutes, or until tender and slightly browned, stirring halfway through.
5. While the vegetables are roasting, pat the salmon fillets dry with paper towels.
6. In a small bowl, whisk together the lemon zest, lemon juice, minced garlic, oregano, thyme, salt, and pepper.
7. Place the salmon fillets on a separate baking sheet lined with parchment paper.
8. Drizzle the marinade over the salmon, ensuring both sides are coated.
9. Bake the salmon for 10-12 minutes, or until cooked through (internal temperature should reach 145°F or 63°C).
10. Divide the roasted vegetables among plates and top with a salmon fillet. Garnish with fresh chopped parsley and a squeeze of lemon juice, if desired.

Tips:

- For a spicier kick, add a pinch of red pepper flakes to the marinade.
- Feel free to substitute other AIP-compliant vegetables, such as carrots, parsnips, or cauliflower florets.
- If you don't have fresh herbs, you can use dried herbs, but use half the amount as they are more concentrated.

I love this recipe because it's so simple to prepare, yet it feels like a gourmet meal. The vibrant colors of the roasted vegetables and the flaky salmon make it visually appealing, while the flavors are simply irresistible.

Indulge in this delicious and nutritious Baked Salmon with Roasted Vegetables as a simple yet satisfying meal on the AIP diet!

"A recipe has no soul. You, as the cook, must bring soul to the recipe." – Thomas Keller

Slow Cooker Beef Stew: Comforting & Flavorful AIP Goodness

Prep Time: 15 minutes **Cook Time:** 6-8 hours on low or 4-5 hours on high **Yields:** 6-8 servings

This hearty and comforting beef stew is a perfect meal for the AIP diet. The slow cooker does all the work, transforming tough cuts of beef into tender morsels, while the vegetables become meltingly soft in a rich and flavorful broth. It's a nourishing and satisfying meal that's ideal for chilly days or for meal prepping.

Ingredients:

- 2 pounds beef stew meat (chuck roast or other stewing cut), cut into 1-inch cubes
- 1/4 cup arrowroot starch or tapioca flour (optional, for thickening)
- 1 tablespoon avocado oil or ghee
- 1 large onion, diced
- 4 cloves garlic, minced
- 3 carrots, peeled and chopped
- 3 stalks celery, chopped
- 1 pound small red potatoes, quartered
- 4 cups beef broth (homemade or store-bought)
- 1 teaspoon dried thyme
- 1 teaspoon dried rosemary
- 1/2 teaspoon sea salt
- 1/4 teaspoon black pepper
- 1 bay leaf
- Optional add-ins:
    - 1/2 cup chopped parsnips
    - 1/2 cup chopped turnips
    - 1 cup sliced mushrooms

Instructions:

1. If you want a thicker stew, toss the beef cubes with the arrowroot starch or tapioca flour in a bowl.
2. Heat the avocado oil or ghee in a large skillet over medium-high heat.
3. Brown the beef cubes in batches, about 2-3 minutes per side.
4. Transfer the browned beef to the slow cooker.
5. In the same skillet, add the onion, garlic, carrots, and celery.
6. Cook for 5-7 minutes, or until the vegetables are softened.
7. Transfer the sautéed vegetables to the slow cooker with the beef.
8. Add the potatoes, beef broth, thyme, rosemary, salt, pepper, and bay leaf.
9. If desired, add any optional vegetables.
10. Cover and cook on low for 6-8 hours, or on high for 4-5 hours, or until the beef is tender and the vegetables are soft.
11. Remove the bay leaf before serving. Ladle the stew into bowls and enjoy!

Tips:

- For a richer flavor, use homemade bone broth made from beef bones.
- Feel free to adjust the amount of vegetables to your preference.
- If you want a thicker stew, you can make a slurry by whisking together 1 tablespoon of arrowroot starch or tapioca flour with 2 tablespoons of cold water. Stir the slurry into the stew during the last 30 minutes of cooking.
- Leftover stew can be stored in the refrigerator for up to 5 days or frozen for later.

I love making this stew on a chilly winter day. The aroma of the beef and vegetables simmering away in the slow cooker fills the house with warmth and comfort. It's a dish that my whole family enjoys, and it always reminds me of home.

Enjoy this comforting and delicious Slow Cooker Beef Stew as a nourishing and satisfying meal on the AIP diet!

"Healthy eating is not about deprivation; it's about nourishment." – Unknown

Shrimp Scampi with Zucchini Noodles: A Light & Zesty AIP Feast

Prep Time: 10 minutes **Cook Time:** 15 minutes **Yields:** 4 servings

This light and flavorful dish is a delicious and healthy alternative to traditional pasta scampi, perfect for those following the AIP diet. Tender shrimp are sautéed in garlic and olive oil, creating a simple yet satisfying sauce that's tossed with spiralized zucchini noodles (zoodles). It's a quick and easy meal that's packed with nutrients and flavor.

Ingredients:

- 1 pound shrimp, peeled and deveined (wild-caught is best)
- 4 medium zucchini, spiralized or julienned into noodle shapes
- 3 tablespoons avocado oil or ghee
- 4 cloves garlic, minced
- 1/4 cup chopped fresh parsley
- 1/4 cup chopped fresh basil
- Juice of 1 lemon
- 1/4 teaspoon sea salt
- 1/4 teaspoon black pepper
- Pinch of red pepper flakes (optional)

Instructions:

1. If using a spiralizer, create zucchini noodles.
2. If not, use a julienne peeler or knife to cut the zucchini into thin strips resembling noodles. Set aside.
3. Heat 2 tablespoons of avocado oil or ghee in a large skillet over medium-high heat.
4. Add the shrimp and cook for 2-3 minutes per side, or until pink and cooked through.
5. Remove the shrimp from the skillet and set aside.
6. In the same skillet, add the remaining 1 tablespoon of oil or ghee.
7. Add the minced garlic and cook for 30 seconds, or until fragrant.
8. Stir in the parsley, basil, lemon juice, salt, pepper, and red pepper flakes (if using).
9. Add the zucchini noodles to the skillet and toss to coat in the sauce.
10. Cook for 2-3 minutes, or until the noodles are tender-crisp.
11. Return the cooked shrimp to the skillet and toss gently to combine with the noodles and sauce.
12. Serve immediately, garnished with additional fresh herbs, if desired.

Tips:

- For a richer flavor, use a combination of avocado oil and ghee for sautéing.

- Feel free to adjust the amount of garlic and herbs to your liking.
- If you don't have fresh herbs, you can use dried herbs, but use half the amount as they are more concentrated.
- To prevent the zucchini noodles from becoming watery, avoid overcooking them.

I love this dish because it's so light and flavorful, yet it feels incredibly indulgent. The combination of garlic, lemon, and herbs creates a bright and zesty sauce that perfectly complements the tender shrimp and zucchini noodles. It's a quick and easy weeknight meal that my whole family enjoys.

Indulge in this delicious and nutritious Shrimp Scampi with Zucchini Noodles as a light and flavorful meal on the AIP diet!

Turkey Meatballs in Nomato Sauce: AIP Comfort Food at Its Best

Prep Time: 15 minutes **Cook Time:** 30 minutes **Yields:** 4-6 servings

These flavorful and tender turkey meatballs are simmered in a rich and savory "nomato" (no tomato) sauce, making them a perfect comfort food option for those following the AIP diet. The combination of herbs, spices, and vegetables creates a depth of flavor that rivals traditional tomato sauce.

Ingredients:

For the Turkey Meatballs:

- 1 pound ground turkey
- 1/2 cup grated carrot
- 1/4 cup chopped onion
- 1/4 cup chopped fresh parsley
- 1 egg, beaten
- 1/4 cup cassava flour (or arrowroot flour)
- 1/2 teaspoon garlic powder
- 1/2 teaspoon dried oregano
- 1/4 teaspoon sea salt
- 1/4 teaspoon black pepper

For the Nomato Sauce (Elimination Phase):

- 1 tablespoon avocado oil or ghee
- 1 medium onion, diced
- 2 cloves garlic, minced
- 2 cups peeled and diced carrots
- 1 medium beet, peeled and diced
- 1/2 cup chopped celery
- 1/2 cup chopped parsnips
- 1/4 teaspoon dried thyme
- 1/4 teaspoon dried rosemary
- 1/4 teaspoon sea salt
- 1/4 teaspoon black pepper
- 1 bay leaf
- 4 cups bone broth (or vegetable broth)
- 1 tablespoon lemon juice

For the Nomato Sauce (Reintroduction Phase):

- Replace the carrots, beets, celery, and parsnips with:
  - 1 (28-ounce) can crushed tomatoes
  - 1/2 teaspoon dried basil

Instructions:

1. In a large bowl, combine all the meatball ingredients.
2. Mix well until everything is evenly combined.
3. Roll the mixture into 1-inch meatballs and set aside.
4. Heat the avocado oil or ghee in a large skillet or pot over medium heat.
5. Add the diced onion and cook until softened, about 5 minutes. Add the minced garlic and cook for another minute, until fragrant.
6. **(Elimination Phase) Add vegetables and broth:** Add the

diced carrots, beets, celery, parsnips, thyme, rosemary, salt, pepper, and bay leaf to the skillet.
7. Pour in the bone broth and lemon juice.
8. Bring to a simmer and cook for 30 minutes, or until the vegetables are tender and the sauce has thickened.
9. **(Reintroduction Phase) Add tomatoes and basil:** Add the crushed tomatoes and basil to the skillet.
10. Bring to a simmer and cook for 15 minutes, or until the sauce has thickened.
11. Gently add the meatballs to the sauce.
12. Reduce heat to low, cover, and simmer for 15-20 minutes, or until the meatballs are cooked through.
13. Serve the meatballs and sauce over zucchini noodles, spaghetti squash, or your favorite AIP-compliant side dish.

Tips:

- If you're short on time, you can use pre-made meatballs (AIP-compliant) and simply simmer them in the nomato sauce.
- For a smoother sauce, use an immersion blender or carefully transfer the sauce to a blender and puree until smooth before returning to the pot.
- Feel free to adjust the seasonings to your taste.

I love making these turkey meatballs for a quick and easy weeknight meal. The nomato sauce is so flavorful and hearty, and the meatballs are always juicy and tender. It's a dish that my whole family enjoys, even those who aren't following AIP.

"Cooking is all about people. Food is maybe the only universal thing that really has the power to bring everyone together. No matter what culture, everywhere around the world, people eat together." - Guy Fieri

Pork Chops with Caramelized Apples & Onions: A Sweet & Savory AIP Delight

Prep Time: 10 minutes **Cook Time:** 25 minutes **Yields:** 4 servings

This elegant yet simple dish is a perfect example of how delicious and satisfying AIP meals can be. The juicy, pan-seared pork chops are beautifully complemented by the sweetness of caramelized apples and onions, creating a symphony of flavors that's both comforting and sophisticated.

Ingredients:

- 4 boneless pork chops (about 1 inch thick)
- 1 tablespoon avocado oil or ghee
- 1 large apple (Honeycrisp or Granny Smith), cored and thinly sliced
- 1 large yellow onion, thinly sliced
- 1/4 cup apple cider vinegar
- 1 tablespoon honey or maple syrup (optional)
- 1/2 teaspoon dried thyme
- 1/4 teaspoon sea salt
- 1/4 teaspoon black pepper
- Fresh chopped parsley, for garnish

Instructions:

1. Pat the pork chops dry with paper towels.
2. Season both sides generously with salt and pepper.
3. Heat the avocado oil or ghee in a large skillet over medium-high heat.
4. Add the pork chops and cook for 4-5 minutes per side, or until browned and cooked through.
5. Remove the pork chops from the skillet and set aside.
6. Add the sliced apples and onions to the skillet.
7. Cook for 8-10 minutes, stirring occasionally, until they are softened and caramelized.
8. Pour in the apple cider vinegar and scrape up any browned bits from the bottom of the skillet.
9. Stir in the honey or maple syrup (if using) and thyme.
10. Return the pork chops to the skillet and cook for an additional 2-3 minutes, or until heated through and the sauce has thickened slightly.
11. Transfer the pork chops to plates and top with the caramelized apples and onions.
12. Garnish with fresh chopped parsley and serve immediately.

Tips:

- For a richer flavor, use bone-in pork chops.
- Feel free to adjust the amount of honey or maple syrup to your liking. If you prefer a less sweet dish, you can omit it altogether.
- You can substitute other AIP-compliant sweeteners, such as date paste or mashed banana, for the honey or maple syrup.
- If you don't have fresh thyme, you can use dried thyme, but use half the amount as it's more concentrated.

I love this recipe because it's so elegant and simple, yet it always impresses my dinner guests. The combination of savory pork chops and sweet caramelized apples and onions is a classic flavor pairing that never fails to delight.

Enjoy this delicious and satisfying Pork Chops with Caramelized Apples and Onions as a flavorful and AIP-compliant meal!

AIP Chicken Curry: A Warm & Fragrant Bowl of Comfort

Prep Time: 15 minutes **Cook Time:** 30 minutes **Yields:** 4 servings

This flavorful and aromatic curry is a comforting and satisfying meal for those following the AIP diet. Tender chicken simmers in a creamy coconut milk sauce infused with warm spices and vibrant vegetables. It's a versatile dish that can be served with cauliflower rice, roasted vegetables, or your favorite AIP-compliant side dish.

Ingredients:

- 1 pound boneless, skinless chicken thighs or breasts, cut into bite-sized pieces
- 1 tablespoon avocado oil or ghee
- 1 medium onion, diced
- 2 cloves garlic, minced
- 1-inch piece of fresh ginger, grated or minced
- 1 tablespoon AIP-compliant curry powder (check for nightshades or seed-based spices)
- 1 teaspoon ground turmeric
- 1/2 teaspoon sea salt
- 1/4 teaspoon black pepper
- 1 (14-ounce) can full-fat coconut milk
- 1 cup chicken broth
- 1 cup chopped vegetables (broccoli florets, cauliflower florets, carrots, zucchini, etc.)
- Optional add-ins:
  - 1/2 cup chopped fresh cilantro, for garnish
  - 1/4 cup chopped fresh mint, for garnish
  - Lime wedges, for serving

Instructions:

1. Heat the avocado oil or ghee in a large skillet or pot over medium heat.
2. Add the diced onion and cook until softened, about 5 minutes.
3. Add the minced garlic and grated ginger and cook for an additional minute, until fragrant.
4. Stir in the curry powder and turmeric.
5. Cook for 1 minute, stirring constantly, until fragrant.
6. Add the chicken pieces to the skillet and cook until browned on all sides.
7. Add the coconut milk and chicken broth to the skillet. Bring to a simmer.
8. Add the chopped vegetables to the skillet.
9. Cover and simmer for 15-20 minutes, or until the chicken is cooked through and the vegetables are tender.
10. Stir in the salt and pepper. Taste and adjust seasonings as needed.
11. Serve warm, garnished with fresh cilantro and mint, if desired, and a squeeze of lime.

Tips:

- For a richer and creamier curry, use full-fat coconut milk.
- Feel free to adjust the amount of spices to your liking. If you prefer a milder curry, reduce the amount of curry powder.
- If you're in the elimination phase, be sure to choose a curry powder that does not contain nightshades or seed-based spices.
- You can make this recipe in a slow cooker by following the same instructions but cooking on low for 4-6 hours or high for 2-3 hours.
- Serve with cauliflower rice or roasted vegetables for a complete AIP meal.

I love making this curry because it's so versatile and customizable. I can change up the vegetables depending on what I have on hand, and I can adjust the spice level to suit my mood. It's a comforting and flavorful meal that's always a hit with my family and friends.

Enjoy this fragrant and flavorful AIP Chicken Curry as a healthy and satisfying meal!

Roasted Butternut Squash Soup: Autumn in a Bowl (AIP-Friendly)

Prep Time: 15 minutes **Cook Time:** 45 minutes **Yields:** 4-6 servings

This creamy and comforting soup is a perfect embodiment of fall flavors, and it's entirely AIP-compliant. Roasting the butternut squash brings out its natural sweetness, while the addition of warm spices and a touch of coconut milk creates a luxurious and satisfying texture. It's a simple yet elegant dish that's perfect for chilly evenings or as a starter for a festive meal.

Ingredients:

- 1 large butternut squash, peeled, seeded, and cubed
- 1 large apple, peeled, cored, and chopped (Honeycrisp or Granny Smith)
- 1 medium yellow onion, chopped
- 3 cloves garlic, minced
- 2 tablespoons avocado oil or ghee
- 4 cups bone broth (homemade or store-bought)
- 1/2 teaspoon ground cinnamon
- 1/4 teaspoon ground nutmeg
- 1/4 teaspoon ground ginger
- 1/4 teaspoon sea salt
- 1/4 teaspoon black pepper
- 1/2 cup full-fat coconut milk
- Optional garnishes: roasted pumpkin seeds, fresh sage leaves, a drizzle of olive oil

Instructions:

1. Preheat oven to 400°F (200°C).
2. Toss the butternut squash, apple, onion, and garlic with avocado oil or ghee, salt, and pepper on a baking sheet.
3. Roast for 30-40 minutes, or until the vegetables are tender and slightly caramelized.
4. Transfer the roasted vegetables to a large pot or Dutch oven.
5. Add the bone broth, cinnamon, nutmeg, ginger, salt, and pepper.
6. Bring to a simmer and cook for 10-15 minutes to allow the flavors to meld.
7. Remove the pot from the heat and carefully transfer the soup to a blender.
8. Blend until smooth and creamy. (Alternatively, you can use an immersion blender directly in the pot.)
9. Return the soup to the pot and stir in the coconut milk.
10. Heat gently over low heat, stirring occasionally, until warmed through.
11. Ladle into bowls and garnish with roasted pumpkin seeds, fresh sage leaves, and a drizzle of olive oil, if desired.

Tips:

- For a richer flavor, use homemade bone broth instead of store-bought.

- Feel free to adjust the amount of spices to your liking.
- If you don't have an apple, you can omit it or substitute with another AIP-compliant fruit, such as pear or cranberries.
- Leftover soup can be stored in the refrigerator for up to 5 days or frozen for later.

I love making this soup in the fall when butternut squash is in season. The warm, comforting flavors always remind me of cozy evenings spent with family and friends. It's a simple yet elegant dish that's perfect for any occasion.

Enjoy this delicious and nourishing Roasted Butternut Squash Soup as a healthy and satisfying meal on the AIP diet!

Beef and Broccoli Stir-Fry: A Flavorful AIP Classic

Prep Time: 15 minutes **Cook Time:** 20 minutes **Yields:** 4 servings

This quick and easy stir-fry is a delicious and satisfying meal for those following the AIP diet. Tender strips of beef are cooked with crisp broccoli florets in a savory sauce made with coconut aminos and ginger. It's a simple yet flavorful dish that's perfect for busy weeknights.

Ingredients:

- 1 pound flank steak or sirloin steak, thinly sliced against the grain
- 1 tablespoon avocado oil or ghee
- 1 large head broccoli, cut into florets
- 1/2 cup coconut aminos
- 1/4 cup bone broth or water
- 2 tablespoons apple cider vinegar (or lime juice)
- 1 tablespoon arrowroot powder or tapioca starch
- 2 cloves garlic, minced
- 1 tablespoon grated fresh ginger (or 1 teaspoon ginger powder)
- 1/2 teaspoon sea salt
- 1/4 teaspoon black pepper
- Optional garnishes: chopped green onions, sesame seeds (if tolerated), sliced avocado

Instructions:

1. In a bowl, combine the sliced beef with half of the coconut aminos, garlic, ginger, salt, and pepper. Let it marinate for 15 minutes.
2. While the beef is marinating, steam or blanch the broccoli florets until tender-crisp, about 3-5 minutes.
3. Drain and set aside.
4. In a small bowl, whisk together the remaining coconut aminos, bone broth or water, apple cider vinegar,

and arrowroot powder or tapioca starch.
5. Heat the avocado oil or ghee in a large skillet or wok over medium-high heat.
6. Add the marinated beef and stir-fry for 3-5 minutes, or until browned.
7. Remove the beef from the skillet and set aside.
8. Add the broccoli florets to the skillet and stir-fry for 2-3 minutes, or until heated through.
9. Pour the sauce into the skillet and bring to a simmer.
10. Add the cooked beef back to the skillet and stir until the sauce has thickened and everything is heated through.
11. Serve immediately over cauliflower rice or with your favorite AIP-compliant side dish.
12. Garnish with chopped green onions, sesame seeds (if tolerated), and sliced avocado, if desired.

Tips:

- For a spicier stir-fry, add a pinch of red pepper flakes or a dash of hot sauce to the sauce.
- Feel free to substitute other AIP-compliant vegetables, such as carrots, mushrooms, or snap peas.
- If you don't have arrowroot powder or tapioca starch, you can omit it or use another AIP-compliant thickener, such as mashed sweet potato.

I love this recipe because it's a quick and easy way to enjoy a takeout-style meal at home without the unhealthy ingredients. The beef is tender and flavorful, the broccoli is crisp-tender, and the sauce is savory and satisfying. It's a great meal for busy weeknights when I don't have a lot of time to cook.

Enjoy this delicious and nutritious Beef and Broccoli Stir-Fry as a healthy and satisfying meal on the AIP diet!

Snacks

"Eating healthy doesn't have to be boring. With a little creativity, you can make delicious and nutritious snacks that fuel your body and soul." – Unknown

Fruit with Almond Butter (AIP Reintroduction Phase): A Simple & Satisfying Snack

Prep Time: 5 minutes **Yields:** 1 serving

This classic combination of fruit and almond butter is a delicious and nutritious snack for those in the reintroduction phase of the AIP diet. The natural sweetness of the fruit pairs perfectly with the creamy, nutty flavor of almond butter, providing a satisfying balance of carbohydrates, healthy fats, and protein.

Ingredients:

- Your choice of AIP-compliant fruit:
    - 1 apple, sliced
    - 1 banana, sliced
    - 1/2 cup berries (strawberries, blueberries, raspberries)
    - Other seasonal fruits like pears, peaches, or plums
- 2 tablespoons almond butter (make sure it's AIP-compliant, with no added sugar or other ingredients)

Instructions:

1. Wash and slice or chop your chosen fruit.
2. Arrange the fruit on a plate or in a container.
3. Top the fruit with almond butter.
4. You can either spread it on top or serve it on the side for dipping.
5. Enjoy!

Tips:

- For extra flavor and nutrition, sprinkle a pinch of cinnamon or nutmeg on top of the fruit and almond butter.
- If you're sensitive to nuts, start with a small amount of almond butter and gradually increase as tolerated.
- You can also use other nut or seed butters in this recipe, such as cashew butter or sunflower seed butter, if you have successfully reintroduced them into your diet.

Alternatives for the Elimination Phase:

- **Mashed sweet potato or banana with coconut butter**: This combination offers a similar creamy texture and sweetness as almond butter, without the nuts.

- Apple slices with mashed avocado:

I love this snack because it's so easy to throw together and it always satisfies my sweet tooth. I often have a container of sliced apples and almond butter in my fridge for a quick and healthy snack on the go.

Indulge in this simple yet satisfying Fruit with Almond Butter as a healthy and delicious snack on the AIP diet!

"Eat the rainbow!" – Unknown

Veggie Sticks with Guacamole: A Fiesta of Freshness (AIP-Friendly)

Prep Time: 10 minutes **Yields:** 4 servings

This vibrant and flavorful snack is a perfect way to enjoy a variety of colorful vegetables while satisfying your cravings for something creamy and savory. The simple guacamole, made with avocado, lime juice, and fresh herbs, is a delicious and nutritious dip that complements the crisp and crunchy vegetables.

Ingredients:

- For the Guacamole:
    - 2 ripe avocados, pitted and mashed
    - 1/4 cup diced red onion
    - 1/4 cup chopped fresh cilantro
    - 2 tablespoons lime juice
    - 1/2 teaspoon sea salt
    - 1/4 teaspoon black pepper
- For the Veggie Sticks:
    - Assorted AIP-compliant vegetables, such as:
        - Carrots, peeled and cut into sticks
        - Celery stalks, cut into sticks
        - Cucumber, sliced
        - Bell peppers (if tolerated during reintroduction), sliced
        - Broccoli florets
        - Cauliflower florets

Instructions:

1. In a medium bowl, combine the mashed avocado, red onion, cilantro, lime juice, salt, and pepper.
2. Mix well until all ingredients are evenly combined.
3. Taste and adjust seasonings as needed.
4. Wash and cut the vegetables into sticks or florets.
5. Arrange them on a platter or individual plates.
6. Serve the guacamole alongside the veggie sticks.
7. Enjoy the fresh, crisp vegetables with the creamy and flavorful guacamole.

Tips:

- For a spicier guacamole, add a diced jalapeno pepper (if tolerated).
- If you don't have fresh cilantro, you can use dried cilantro, but use half the amount as it's more concentrated.
- Feel free to experiment with other AIP-compliant herbs and spices in

- the guacamole, such as cumin, paprika, or garlic powder.
- Leftover guacamole can be stored in an airtight container in the refrigerator for up to 2 days. To prevent browning, place a piece of plastic wrap directly on the surface of the guacamole before sealing the container.

I love this snack because it's so easy to put together and it's always a hit at gatherings. It's a great way to get my daily dose of vegetables, and the creamy guacamole makes it feel like a real treat.

Embrace the vibrant colors and flavors of this delicious and nutritious Veggie Sticks with Guacamole as a healthy and satisfying snack on the AIP diet.

"Eating healthy food fills your body with energy and nutrients. Imagine your cells smiling back at you and saying: 'Thank you!'" - Karen Salmansohn

Hard-Boiled Eggs (AIP Reintroduction Phase): Protein Powerhouses in a Shell

Prep Time: 5 minutes **Cook Time:** 10-12 minutes **Yields:** Varies depending on the number of eggs

Hard-boiled eggs are a classic, convenient, and nutritious snack or addition to meals, especially for those following the AIP diet. They're packed with protein, essential vitamins, and minerals, making them a great way to stay fueled and energized throughout the day.

Ingredients:

- Eggs (as many as you like)
- Water

Instructions:

1. Arrange the eggs in a single layer at the bottom of a saucepan.
2. Add enough cold water to cover the eggs by about an inch.
3. Place the saucepan over high heat and bring the water to a rolling boil.
4. Once the water has reached a full boil, turn off the heat and cover the saucepan with a lid.
5. Let the eggs sit in the hot water for the desired cooking time:
   - 10 minutes for slightly soft yolks
   - 12 minutes for fully cooked yolks
6. After the desired cooking time, drain the hot water and run cold water over the eggs to stop the cooking process.
7. Gently tap each egg on a hard surface to crack the shell, then peel under cold running water.

Tips:

- Adding a teaspoon of salt or baking soda to the water can help prevent the eggs from cracking and make them easier to peel.
- To make peeling easier, cool the eggs in an ice bath for a few minutes after draining the hot water.
- Store hard-boiled eggs in the refrigerator for up to 5 days.

AIP Elimination Phase Note:

Eggs are typically eliminated during the initial phase of the AIP diet due to their potential allergenic properties. However, they are a nutrient-dense food and can be reintroduced after a few weeks, depending on individual tolerance.

I remember being hesitant to reintroduce eggs into my AIP diet, but once I did, I was pleasantly surprised at how well I tolerated them. Now, hard-boiled eggs are one of my favorite grab-and-go snacks. They're perfect for curbing hunger between meals or adding a boost of protein to salads and bowls.

Enjoy these simple and versatile hard-boiled eggs as a nutritious and satisfying snack or addition to your AIP meals!

"Healthy eating is not about deprivation; it's about nourishment." - Unknown

Baked Plantain Chips: A Crispy & Savory AIP Snack

Prep Time: 10 minutes **Cook Time:** 20-25 minutes **Yields:** 4 servings

These crispy and flavorful plantain chips are a satisfying and healthy alternative to traditional potato chips, perfect for the AIP diet. Made with just a few simple ingredients, they're easy to make and packed with nutrients. Enjoy them on their own or with your favorite AIP-compliant dip.

Ingredients:

- 2 green plantains
- 2 tablespoons avocado oil
- 1/2 teaspoon sea salt
- Optional spices:
    - Garlic powder
    - Onion powder
    - Paprika
    - Chili powder

Instructions:

1. Preheat your oven to 400°F (200°C).

2. Line a baking sheet with parchment paper.
3. Peel the plantains. This can be tricky, so here's a tip: cut off the ends, score the skin lengthwise, and then gently peel it away.
4. Slice the plantains thinly using a mandoline or a sharp knife (aim for 1/8-inch thick slices).
5. In a large bowl, toss the plantain slices with avocado oil, salt, and any desired spices.
6. Arrange the plantain slices in a single layer on the prepared baking sheet.
7. Bake for 20-25 minutes, or until golden brown and crispy, flipping halfway through.
8. Let the plantain chips cool completely on the baking sheet before serving.
9. They will continue to crisp up as they cool.

Tips:

- For even crispier chips, you can bake them for a few extra minutes, but keep a close eye on them to prevent burning.
- The chips are best enjoyed fresh, but they can be stored in an airtight container at room temperature for up to 2 days.

I used to love potato chips before starting the AIP diet, but these plantain chips have become a delicious and satisfying substitute. I love the way they get crispy in the oven, and the combination of sweet and salty flavors is so addictive!

Indulge in these crispy and flavorful Baked Plantain Chips as a healthy and satisfying snack on the AIP diet!

"Eating a rainbow of fruits and vegetables is a delicious way to nourish your body and soul." - Unknown

Rainbow Fruit Salad: A Burst of AIP-Friendly Sunshine

Prep Time: 10 minutes **Yields:** 4 servings

This refreshing and flavorful fruit salad is a perfect way to enjoy the abundance of seasonal fruits on the AIP diet. The combination of vibrant colors, textures, and tastes makes it a delightful and nutritious snack or dessert.

Ingredients:

- 2 cups of your favorite AIP-compliant fruits, such as:
    - 1 cup diced mango
    - 1 cup sliced strawberries
    - 1/2 cup blueberries

- - 1/2 cup raspberries
  - 1/2 cup chopped pineapple
  - 1/2 cup diced honeydew melon
  - Other seasonal fruits like grapes, pears, or apricots
- Optional additions:
  - 1 tablespoon fresh lime juice
  - 1/4 cup shredded coconut (unsweetened)
  - A few fresh mint leaves, chopped

Instructions:

1. Wash and chop all the fruits into bite-sized pieces.
2. In a large bowl, combine all the chopped fruits.
3. If desired, sprinkle the lime juice over the fruit and toss gently.
4. Top with shredded coconut and chopped mint leaves, if using.
5. Enjoy immediately or chill in the refrigerator for a refreshing snack or dessert.

Tips:

- Use a variety of colors and textures to make your fruit salad visually appealing.
- Choose fruits that are in season for the best flavor and freshness.
- If you're not using the fruit salad right away, toss it with a bit of lemon or lime juice to prevent browning.
- Feel free to adjust the amount of fruit and toppings to your liking

I love making this fruit salad as a healthy and refreshing snack or dessert. It's so easy to throw together, and the vibrant colors and flavors always brighten up my day. I especially love adding a sprinkle of shredded coconut and a few chopped mint leaves for an extra touch of tropical flavor.

Indulge in this vibrant and refreshing Rainbow Fruit Salad as a healthy and satisfying snack or dessert on the AIP diet!

"Healthy eating is not about deprivation; it's about nourishment." - Unknown

Coconut Yogurt with Berries: A Tropical Delight (AIP-Friendly)

Prep Time: 5 minutes (plus yogurt culturing time, if making homemade)
Yields: 2 servings

This creamy and tangy coconut yogurt, topped with vibrant berries, is a refreshing and healthy snack or dessert on the AIP diet. The probiotic-rich yogurt is made with simple ingredients and can be enjoyed with a variety of seasonal fruits.

Ingredients:

- 1 cup plain, unsweetened coconut yogurt (store-bought or homemade)
- 1 cup mixed berries (strawberries, blueberries, raspberries, blackberries)
- Optional toppings:
    - 1 tablespoon shredded coconut (unsweetened)
    - A few chopped mint leaves

Instructions:

1. If making your own coconut yogurt, follow a trusted AIP-compliant recipe.
2. Allow the yogurt to culture for 24-48 hours for optimal flavor and probiotic content.
3. Divide the coconut yogurt between two bowls or jars.
4. Top the yogurt with the mixed berries.
5. If desired, sprinkle with shredded coconut and chopped mint leaves.
6. Enjoy immediately or chill in the refrigerator for a cooler treat.

Tips:

- For a smoother yogurt, use full-fat coconut milk when making it at home.
- You can adjust the amount of berries to your liking.
- Feel free to experiment with other AIP-compliant fruits, such as chopped mango, pineapple, or kiwi.

Making Homemade Coconut Yogurt (AIP-Friendly):

Ingredients:

- 1 (14-ounce) can full-fat coconut milk
- 2 probiotic capsules (choose a brand with dairy-free strains)

Instructions:

1. Pour the coconut milk into a saucepan and heat over low heat until it's warm to the touch (not boiling).
2. Remove from heat and let cool to 100-110°F (38-43°C).
3. Open the probiotic capsules and stir the contents into the coconut milk.
4. Pour the mixture into a clean glass jar and cover with a cheesecloth or a clean kitchen towel.
5. Secure with a rubber band. Place the jar in a warm spot (70-80°F or 21-27°C) for 24-48 hours, or until the yogurt thickens and has a tangy flavor.
6. Once the yogurt is set, transfer it to the refrigerator and chill for at least 2 hours before serving.

I've always loved yogurt, but finding a dairy-free version that was AIP-compliant was a challenge. Making my own coconut yogurt opened up a world of delicious possibilities, and I love experimenting with different fruits and toppings.

Indulge in this refreshing and nutritious Coconut Yogurt with Berries as a healthy and satisfying snack or dessert on the AIP diet!

"Eating healthy doesn't have to be boring. With a little creativity, you can make delicious and nutritious snacks that satisfy your cravings and nourish your body." - Unknown

Carrot Sticks with "No-Chickpea" Hummus: A Crunchy & Flavorful AIP Snack

Prep Time: 10 minutes **Yields:** 4 servings

This satisfying and nutritious snack is perfect for the AIP diet. Crisp carrot sticks are paired with a creamy and flavorful "no-chickpea" hummus, providing a healthy dose of fiber, vitamins, and minerals.

Ingredients:

- For the AIP "No-Chickpea" Hummus (Elimination Phase):
    - 1 head cauliflower, cut into florets
    - 1/4 cup tahini (sesame seed paste)
    - 2 tablespoons lemon juice
    - 2 tablespoons olive oil
    - 1/2 teaspoon garlic powder
    - 1/4 teaspoon sea salt
    - 1/4 teaspoon black pepper
- For the Carrot Sticks:
    - 4-5 large carrots, peeled and cut into sticks

Instructions:

1. Make the Hummus (Elimination Phase):
    - Steam or roast the cauliflower florets until tender.
    - In a food processor, combine the cooked cauliflower, tahini, lemon juice, olive oil, garlic powder, salt, and pepper.
    - Process until smooth and creamy, scraping down the sides as needed.
    - Taste and adjust seasonings as needed.
2. Wash and peel the carrots.
3. Cut them into sticks of your desired size.
4. Arrange the carrot sticks on a platter or individual plates.
5. Serve with the "no-chickpea" hummus.

Tips:

- For a smoother hummus, add a tablespoon or two of water to the food processor while blending.
- Feel free to add other AIP-compliant spices to the hummus, such as cumin, paprika, or turmeric.
- You can substitute other AIP-compliant vegetables for the carrots, such as celery sticks, cucumber slices, or bell pepper strips (if tolerated).
- Leftover hummus can be stored in an airtight container in the refrigerator for up to 5 days.

Hummus Alternative for Reintroduction Phase:

If you've successfully reintroduced legumes into your AIP diet, you can use canned chickpeas to make traditional hummus. Simply drain and rinse the chickpeas, then blend them with tahini, lemon juice, olive oil, garlic, salt, and pepper until smooth and creamy.

I love this snack because it's so easy to make and it's always a hit with my family. The "no-chickpea" hummus is surprisingly similar to traditional hummus in terms of flavor and texture, and it's a great way to get my kids to eat more vegetables.

Enjoy this healthy and satisfying Carrot Sticks with "No-Chickpea" Hummus as a guilt-free snack on the AIP diet!

"Healthy eating is not about deprivation; it's about nourishment." – Unknown

Baked Sweet Potato Chips: A Sweet & Savory AIP Snack

Prep Time: 10 minutes **Cook Time:** 20-30 minutes **Yields:** 4 servings

These crispy and naturally sweet potato chips are a satisfying and healthy alternative to traditional potato chips, perfect for the AIP diet. They're made with just a few simple ingredients and baked to perfection, making them a guilt-free snack that's packed with nutrients.

Ingredients:

- 2 medium sweet potatoes
- 2 tablespoons avocado oil (or melted coconut oil)
- 1/2 teaspoon sea salt
- Optional spices (to taste):
    - Garlic powder
    - Onion powder
    - Paprika
    - Cayenne pepper (for a spicy kick)

Instructions:

1. Preheat your oven to 400°F (200°C).
2. Line two baking sheets with parchment paper.
3. Wash and peel the sweet potatoes. Using a mandoline or a sharp knife, slice them as thinly as possible (aim for 1/8-inch thick slices). The thinner the slices, the crispier the chips.
4. In a large bowl, toss the sweet potato slices with avocado oil (or melted coconut oil), salt, and any desired spices.
5. Arrange the slices in a single layer on the prepared baking sheets, making sure they don't overlap.
6. Bake for 10 minutes, then flip the chips and bake for an additional 10-20 minutes, or until golden brown and crispy.
7. Keep a close eye on them towards the end, as they can burn easily.
8. Let the sweet potato chips cool completely on the baking sheets. They will continue to crisp up as they cool.

Tips:

- If your sweet potato slices are thicker, they may need to bake for a longer time.
- For extra crispy chips, you can try soaking the sliced sweet potatoes in cold water for 30 minutes before baking. This helps to remove some of the starch, which can prevent them from getting as crispy.
- Store any leftover chips in an airtight container at room temperature.

I used to crave potato chips all the time before I started the AIP diet. These baked sweet potato chips have been a lifesaver! They satisfy my craving for something salty and crunchy, but they're also packed with nutrients and so much better for me than traditional potato chips.

Indulge in these delicious and healthy baked sweet potato chips as a satisfying and guilt-free snack on the AIP diet!

"Healthy eating is not about deprivation; it's about nourishment." - Unknown

Avocado Deviled Eggs: A Creamy & Flavorful AIP Appetizer

Prep Time: 10 minutes **Cook Time:** 10-12 minutes **Yields:** 12 deviled egg halves

These delectable Avocado Deviled Eggs are a healthy and satisfying twist on a classic appetizer, perfect for those following the AIP diet. The creamy avocado filling, infused with zesty lemon and fresh herbs, replaces the traditional mayonnaise for a guilt-free indulgence that's packed with nutrients.

Ingredients:

- 6 hard-boiled eggs
- 1 ripe avocado, pitted and mashed
- 1 tablespoon lemon juice
- 1/4 teaspoon garlic powder
- 1/4 teaspoon onion powder
- 1/4 teaspoon sea salt
- 1/4 teaspoon black pepper
- Pinch of cayenne pepper (optional)
- Chopped fresh herbs (chives, parsley, or dill), for garnish

Instructions:

1. Hard-boil the eggs using your preferred method (see tips below).
2. Once cooked, cool the eggs in an ice bath, peel, and slice in half lengthwise.
3. Carefully scoop out the yolks and place them in a medium bowl.
4. Mash the yolks with a fork until smooth. Add the mashed avocado, lemon juice, garlic powder, onion powder, salt, pepper, and cayenne pepper (if using).
5. Mix well until thoroughly combined.
6. Spoon or pipe the filling back into the egg whites.
7. Garnish with chopped fresh herbs and
8. Serve immediately or chill in the refrigerator for later.

Tips:

- For perfectly cooked hard-boiled eggs, place them in a saucepan and cover with cold water. Bring to a boil, then immediately remove from heat and cover with a lid. Let sit for 12 minutes, then drain and cool in an ice bath. This method prevents the yolks from turning green and makes them easier to peel.
- For a smoother filling, you can use a food processor or immersion blender to combine the ingredients.
- Feel free to adjust the seasonings to your liking.
- For a fun presentation, you can use a piping bag with a decorative tip to fill the egg whites.
- Leftover deviled eggs can be stored in an airtight container in the refrigerator for up to 2 days.

I used to love deviled eggs, but the mayonnaise-heavy filling wasn't AIP-friendly. This avocado version is even more delicious and nutritious, and it's always a hit at parties and potlucks.

Indulge in these creamy and flavorful Avocado Deviled Eggs as a healthy and satisfying appetizer or snack on the AIP diet!

"Healthy eating can be fun and delicious!" - Unknown

Ants on a Log" (AIP-Friendly): A Crunchy & Fun Snack

Prep Time: 5 minutes **Yields:** 2-4 servings (depending on how many "logs" you make)

This classic snack is a fun and easy way to enjoy a combination of flavors and textures on the AIP diet. Celery sticks act as the "logs," filled with a creamy "ant" filling, and topped with sweet "ants."

Ingredients:

- For the "Logs":
    - 4-6 stalks celery, washed and cut into 3-4 inch pieces
- For the "Ants" Filling (Elimination Phase):
    - 1/2 cup mashed banana
    - 1/4 cup coconut butter, softened
    - Optional: A pinch of cinnamon or nutmeg
- For the "Ants" Filling (Reintroduction Phase):
    - 1/4 cup almond butter (or other nut/seed butter, if tolerated)
- For the "Ants" Topping (Reintroduction Phase):
    - 1/4 cup raisins or dried cranberries

Instructions:

1. Wash and cut the celery stalks into 3-4 inch pieces.
2. **Make the filling (Elimination Phase):** In a small bowl, mash the banana with a fork until smooth. Stir in the softened coconut butter and optional spices.
3. **Make the filling (Reintroduction Phase):** If you're in the reintroduction phase and tolerate nuts and seeds, simply use almond butter (or other nut/seed butter) as the filling.
4. Spread a generous amount of the filling into the concave side of each celery stick.
5. **(Reintroduction Phase) Add the topping:** If you're in the reintroduction phase and tolerate dried fruit, top each celery stick with a few raisins or dried cranberries.
6. Enjoy!

Tips:

- For a smoother filling, you can blend the banana and coconut butter in a food processor or blender.
- Feel free to experiment with different spices in the filling, such as cardamom or ginger.
- If you don't have raisins or dried cranberries, you can use other AIP-compliant dried fruit, such as chopped dates or apricots.

I remember making "Ants on a Log" as a kid, and it was always a fun and easy snack. Now, I love making this AIP-friendly version with my kids. It's a great way to get them to eat more vegetables, and they love the playful presentation.

Enjoy this fun and nutritious snack on the AIP diet!

Soups & Stews

"Soup is a lot like a hug in a bowl." - Unknown

Creamy Carrot & Ginger Soup: A Warming Hug for Your Soul (AIP-Friendly)

Prep Time: 10 minutes **Cook Time:** 30 minutes **Yields:** 4-6 servings

This velvety smooth and vibrant soup is a comforting classic for those following the AIP diet. The sweetness of the carrots beautifully balances the warmth of ginger, while the coconut milk adds a luxurious creaminess. It's a nourishing and flavorful meal that's perfect for chilly days or when you're feeling under the weather.

Ingredients:

- 2 tablespoons avocado oil or ghee
- 1 large yellow onion, diced
- 2 cloves garlic, minced
- 1 tablespoon freshly grated ginger (or 1 teaspoon dried ginger)
- 1 pound carrots, peeled and chopped
- 4 cups vegetable broth (or bone broth for extra richness)
- 1 cup full-fat coconut milk (or more, to taste)
- 1/2 teaspoon sea salt
- 1/4 teaspoon black pepper
- Optional garnishes:
    - Chopped fresh cilantro or parsley
    - A swirl of coconut cream
    - A drizzle of olive oil

Instructions:

1. Heat the avocado oil or ghee in a large pot or Dutch oven over medium heat.
2. Add the diced onion and cook until softened and translucent, about 5 minutes.
3. Add the minced garlic and grated ginger, and cook for an additional minute, until fragrant.
4. Add the chopped carrots and vegetable broth (or bone broth) to the pot.
5. Bring to a boil, then reduce heat and simmer until the carrots are tender, about 20 minutes.
6. Remove the pot from the heat and carefully transfer the soup to a blender.
7. Blend until smooth and creamy. (Alternatively, you can use an immersion blender directly in the pot.)
8. Return the soup to the pot and stir in the coconut milk, salt, and pepper.
9. Heat gently over low heat, stirring occasionally, until warmed through.
10. Ladle the soup into bowls. Garnish with chopped cilantro or parsley, a

swirl of coconut cream, and a drizzle of olive oil, if desired.

Tips:

- If you don't have fresh ginger, you can use dried ginger powder, but use a smaller amount as it's more potent.
- Feel free to adjust the amount of coconut milk to achieve your desired consistency.
- For a hint of sweetness, add a teaspoon of honey or maple syrup to the soup.
- Leftover soup can be stored in the refrigerator for up to 5 days or frozen for later.

I love this soup because it's so simple to make, yet incredibly satisfying and nourishing. The warm flavors of ginger and the creamy coconut milk always make me feel comforted and grounded, especially on chilly days. It's a go-to recipe when I'm feeling under the weather or just need a little extra warmth in my life.

Embrace the warmth and comfort of this delicious Creamy Carrot & Ginger Soup as a nourishing and healing addition to your AIP journey.

Chicken Zoodle Soup: Nourishing & Flavorful AIP Comfort

Prep Time: 15 minutes **Cook Time:** 30 minutes **Yields:** 4-6 servings

This comforting and flavorful soup is a delicious and healthy alternative to traditional chicken noodle soup, perfect for those following the AIP diet. Tender chicken and a variety of vegetables simmer in a flavorful broth, while zucchini noodles (zoodles) provide a light and satisfying texture.

Ingredients:

- 2 tablespoons avocado oil or ghee
- 1 large yellow onion, diced
- 2 cloves garlic, minced
- 1-inch piece of fresh ginger, grated or minced (optional)
- 2 carrots, peeled and chopped
- 2 stalks celery, chopped
- 4 cups chicken broth (homemade or store-bought)
- 1 teaspoon dried thyme
- 1/2 teaspoon dried rosemary
- 1/4 teaspoon sea salt
- 1/4 teaspoon black pepper
- 2 cups cooked, shredded chicken (from a rotisserie chicken or leftover roast)
- 2 medium zucchini, spiralized or julienned into noodle shapes
- Optional garnishes:

- Chopped fresh parsley or dill
- A drizzle of olive oil

Instructions:

1. Heat the avocado oil or ghee in a large pot or Dutch oven over medium heat. Add the diced onion and cook until softened, about 5 minutes.
2. Add the minced garlic and grated ginger (if using), and cook for an additional minute, until fragrant.
3. Add the carrots, celery, chicken broth, thyme, rosemary, salt, and pepper to the pot.
4. Bring to a boil, then reduce heat and simmer for 15-20 minutes, or until the vegetables are tender.
5. Add the shredded chicken and zucchini noodles to the pot.
6. Cook for 3-5 minutes, or until the noodles are tender-crisp.
7. Ladle the soup into bowls and garnish with fresh parsley or dill and a drizzle of olive oil, if desired.

Tips:

- For a richer flavor, use homemade bone broth made from chicken bones.
- Feel free to add other AIP-compliant vegetables, such as chopped kale or spinach.
- If you don't have a spiralizer, you can use a vegetable peeler or julienne peeler to create zucchini noodles.
- Leftover soup can be stored in the refrigerator for up to 5 days or frozen for later.

I've always loved chicken noodle soup, but the traditional noodles weren't AIP-friendly. When I discovered zucchini noodles (zoodles), it opened up a whole new world of possibilities for me. This zoodle soup is just as comforting and satisfying as the original, but it's much healthier and easier on my digestion.

Embrace the warmth and comfort of this delicious Chicken Zoodle Soup as a nourishing and healing meal on the AIP diet!

Roasted Butternut Squash Soup: Autumn in a Bowl (AIP-Friendly)

Prep Time: 15 minutes **Cook Time:** 45 minutes **Yields:** 4-6 servings

This creamy and comforting soup is a perfect embodiment of fall flavors, and it's entirely AIP-compliant. Roasting the butternut squash brings out its natural sweetness, while the addition of warm spices and a touch of coconut milk creates a luxurious and satisfying texture. It's a simple yet elegant dish that's perfect for chilly evenings or as a starter for a festive meal.

Ingredients:

- 1 large butternut squash, peeled, seeded, and cubed
- 1 large apple, peeled, cored, and chopped (Honeycrisp or Granny Smith)
- 1 medium yellow onion, chopped
- 3 cloves garlic, minced
- 2 tablespoons avocado oil or ghee
- 4 cups bone broth (homemade or store-bought)
- 1 teaspoon ground cinnamon
- 1/4 teaspoon ground nutmeg
- 1/4 teaspoon ground ginger
- 1/4 teaspoon sea salt
- 1/4 teaspoon black pepper
- 1/2 cup full-fat coconut milk
- Optional garnishes: roasted pumpkin seeds, fresh sage leaves, a drizzle of olive oil

Instructions:

1. Preheat oven to 400°F (200°C).
2. Toss the butternut squash, apple, onion, and garlic with avocado oil or ghee, salt, and pepper on a baking sheet.
3. Roast for 30-40 minutes, or until the vegetables are tender and slightly caramelized.
4. Transfer the roasted vegetables to a large pot or Dutch oven.
5. Add the bone broth, cinnamon, nutmeg, ginger, salt, and pepper.
6. Bring to a simmer and cook for 10-15 minutes to allow the flavors to meld.
7. Remove the pot from the heat and carefully transfer the soup to a blender.
8. Blend until smooth and creamy. (Alternatively, you can use an immersion blender directly in the pot.)
9. Return the soup to the pot and stir in the coconut milk.
10. Heat gently over low heat, stirring occasionally, until warmed through.
11. Ladle into bowls and garnish with roasted pumpkin seeds, fresh sage leaves, and a drizzle of olive oil, if desired.

Tips:

- For a richer flavor, use homemade bone broth instead of store-bought.

- Feel free to adjust the amount of spices to your liking.
- If you don't have an apple, you can omit it or substitute with another AIP-compliant fruit, such as pear or cranberries.
- Leftover soup can be stored in the refrigerator for up to 5 days or frozen for later.

I love making this soup in the fall when butternut squash is in season. The warm, comforting flavors always remind me of cozy evenings spent with family and friends. It's a simple yet elegant dish that's perfect for any occasion.

Enjoy this delicious and nourishing Roasted Butternut Squash Soup as a healthy and satisfying meal on the AIP diet!

Crockpot Beef Stew: Comforting Warmth Made Easy (AIP-Friendly)

Prep Time: 15 minutes **Cook Time:** 6-8 hours on low or 4-5 hours on high **Yields:** 6-8 servings

This hearty and nourishing beef stew is a quintessential comfort food made even easier with the help of your trusty crockpot. Tender chunks of beef simmer slowly with vegetables in a flavorful broth, creating a satisfying and nutritious meal that's perfect for chilly days or meal prepping.

Ingredients:

- 2 pounds beef stew meat (chuck roast or other stewing cut), cut into 1-inch cubes
- 1/4 cup arrowroot starch or tapioca flour (optional, for thickening)
- 1 tablespoon avocado oil or ghee
- 1 large onion, diced
- 4 cloves garlic, minced
- 3 carrots, peeled and chopped
- 3 stalks celery, chopped
- 1 pound small red potatoes, quartered
- 4 cups beef broth (homemade or store-bought)
- 1 teaspoon dried thyme
- 1 teaspoon dried rosemary
- 1/2 teaspoon sea salt
- 1/4 teaspoon black pepper
- 1 bay leaf

Optional Add-ins (Reintroduction Phase):

- 1/2 cup chopped parsnips
- 1/2 cup chopped turnips
- 1 cup sliced mushrooms
- 1/4 cup dry red wine (if tolerated)

Instructions:

1. **Optional**: If you want a thicker stew, toss the beef cubes with the arrowroot starch or tapioca flour in a bowl.

2. Heat the avocado oil or ghee in a large skillet over medium-high heat.
3. Brown the beef cubes in batches, about 2-3 minutes per side.
4. Transfer the browned beef to the slow cooker.
5. In the same skillet, add the onion, garlic, carrots, and celery.
6. Cook for 5-7 minutes, or until the vegetables are softened.
7. Transfer the sautéed vegetables to the slow cooker with the beef.
8. Add the potatoes, beef broth, thyme, rosemary, salt, pepper, and bay leaf.
9. If you're in the reintroduction phase and tolerating them, you can add the optional vegetables and red wine.
10. Cover and cook on low for 6-8 hours, or on high for 4-5 hours, or until the beef is tender and the vegetables are soft.
11. Remove the bay leaf before serving. Ladle the stew into bowls and enjoy!

Tips:

- For a richer flavor, use homemade bone broth made from beef bones.
- Feel free to adjust the amount of vegetables to your preference.
- If you want a thicker stew without using arrowroot or tapioca, you can remove some of the broth after cooking, blend it until smooth, and then stir it back into the stew.
- Leftover stew can be stored in the refrigerator for up to 5 days or frozen for later.

I love making this stew on a Sunday afternoon. The aroma that fills the house as it cooks all day is irresistible. It's a warm and comforting meal that's perfect for sharing with family and friends.

Enjoy this delicious and easy Crockpot Beef Stew as a satisfying and AIP-compliant

Hearty Turkey Vegetable Soup: Comforting & Nourishing AIP Goodness

Prep Time: 15 minutes **Cook Time:** 30-45 minutes **Yields:** 6-8 servings

This hearty and flavorful soup is a perfect meal for those following the AIP diet. It's packed with tender turkey, a medley of colorful vegetables, and aromatic herbs, all simmered in a flavorful broth. This soup is not only delicious and satisfying but also incredibly nourishing, making it a great choice for chilly days or when you're feeling under the weather.

Ingredients:

- 2 tablespoons avocado oil or ghee
- 1 large yellow onion, diced
- 2 cloves garlic, minced

- 1-inch piece of fresh ginger, grated or minced (optional)
- 3 carrots, peeled and chopped
- 3 stalks celery, chopped
- 1 pound small red potatoes, quartered
- 4 cups turkey or chicken bone broth (homemade or store-bought)
- 1 teaspoon dried thyme
- 1/2 teaspoon dried rosemary
- 1/4 teaspoon sea salt
- 1/4 teaspoon black pepper
- 2 cups cooked, shredded turkey (from a leftover roast or rotisserie chicken)
- Optional add-ins:
    - 1/2 cup chopped parsnips
    - 1/2 cup chopped turnips
    - 1 cup sliced mushrooms
    - 1/2 cup chopped kale or spinach
    - 1/4 cup chopped fresh parsley, for garnish

Instructions:

1. Heat the avocado oil or ghee in a large pot or Dutch oven over medium heat.
2. Add the diced onion and cook until softened, about 5 minutes.
3. Add the minced garlic and grated ginger (if using), and cook for an additional minute, until fragrant.
4. Add the carrots, celery, potatoes, and any optional vegetables (parsnips, turnips, or mushrooms) to the pot.
5. Cook for 5-7 minutes, stirring occasionally.
6. Pour in the turkey or chicken bone broth, thyme, rosemary, salt, and pepper.
7. Bring to a boil, then reduce heat and simmer for 15-20 minutes, or until the vegetables are tender.
8. Stir in the shredded turkey and cook for an additional 5 minutes, or until heated through.
9. **Optional greens**: If using kale or spinach, add it during the last 2-3 minutes of cooking, just until wilted.
10. Ladle the soup into bowls and garnish with fresh parsley, if desired.

Tips:

- For a richer flavor, use homemade bone broth made from turkey or chicken bones.
- Feel free to adjust the amount and type of vegetables to your preference.
- If you don't have fresh herbs, you can use dried herbs, but use half the amount as they are more concentrated.
- Leftover soup can be stored in the refrigerator for up to 5 days or frozen for later.

I love making a big batch of this soup on a Sunday afternoon. The aroma that fills the house as it simmers is so comforting and inviting. It's a hearty and satisfying meal that's perfect for sharing with family and friends.

Enjoy this delicious and nourishing Turkey Vegetable Soup as a healthy and satisfying meal on the AIP diet!

Curried Cauliflower Soup: A Flavorful and Aromatic AIP Delight

Prep Time: 10 minutes **Cook Time:** 30 minutes **Yields:** 4 servings

This creamy and fragrant soup is a delicious and satisfying way to enjoy cauliflower on the AIP diet. The combination of warming curry spices, rich coconut milk, and tender cauliflower florets creates a comforting and flavorful meal that's perfect for chilly days or when you're craving something exotic.

Ingredients:

- 1 head cauliflower, cut into florets
- 1 tablespoon avocado oil or ghee
- 1 medium yellow onion, diced
- 2 cloves garlic, minced
- 1-inch piece of fresh ginger, grated or minced (or 1 teaspoon ginger powder)
- 1 tablespoon AIP-compliant curry powder (check for nightshades or seed-based spices)
- 1 teaspoon ground turmeric
- 1/2 teaspoon sea salt
- 1/4 teaspoon black pepper
- 4 cups vegetable broth (or bone broth for extra richness)
- 1 (14-ounce) can full-fat coconut milk
- Optional garnishes:
  - Chopped fresh cilantro
  - A swirl of coconut cream
  - A drizzle of olive oil

Instructions:

1. **Sauté the aromatics:** Heat the avocado oil or ghee in a large pot or Dutch oven over medium heat.
2. Add the diced onion and cook until softened, about 5 minutes.
3. Add the minced garlic and grated ginger (or ginger powder), and cook for an additional minute, until fragrant.
4. Stir in the curry powder and turmeric.
5. Cook for 1 minute, stirring constantly, until fragrant.
6. Add the cauliflower florets and vegetable broth (or bone broth) to the pot.
7. Bring to a boil, then reduce heat and simmer until the cauliflower is tender, about 15-20 minutes.

8. Remove the pot from the heat and carefully transfer the soup to a blender.
9. Blend until smooth and creamy. (Alternatively, you can use an immersion blender directly in the pot.)
10. Return the soup to the pot and stir in the coconut milk, salt, and pepper.
11. Heat gently over low heat, stirring occasionally, until warmed through.
12. Ladle the soup into bowls and garnish with chopped cilantro, a swirl of coconut cream, and a drizzle of olive oil, if desired.

Tips:

- For a richer and creamier soup, use full-fat coconut milk.
- Feel free to adjust the amount of spices to your liking. If you prefer a milder curry, reduce the amount of curry powder.
- If you're in the elimination phase, be sure to choose a curry powder that does not contain nightshades or seed-based spices.
- You can add other AIP-compliant vegetables, such as carrots or sweet potatoes, for added flavor and nutrition.

I love this soup because it's a quick and easy way to transform ordinary cauliflower into a flavorful and exotic dish. The warm spices and creamy coconut milk create a comforting and satisfying meal that's perfect for any time of year.

Enjoy this delicious and nourishing Curried Cauliflower Soup as a healthy and satisfying meal on the AIP diet!

Broccoli and Kale Soup: A Vibrant & Nourishing AIP Elixir

Prep Time: 10 minutes **Cook Time:** 25 minutes **Yields:** 4-6 servings

This vibrant green soup is a powerhouse of nutrients, making it a delicious and healthy addition to your AIP meal plan. The combination of broccoli and kale, both cruciferous vegetables packed with vitamins, minerals, and antioxidants, creates a flavorful and satisfying soup that's perfect for any time of year.

Ingredients:

- 2 tablespoons avocado oil or ghee
- 1 large yellow onion, diced
- 2 cloves garlic, minced
- 1 head broccoli, cut into florets
- 1 bunch kale, stems removed and chopped
- 4 cups vegetable broth (or bone broth for extra richness)
- 1 teaspoon dried thyme
- 1/2 teaspoon dried oregano
- 1/4 teaspoon sea salt
- 1/4 teaspoon black pepper
- 1/2 cup full-fat coconut milk (optional, for creaminess)
- Optional garnishes:
  - Chopped fresh parsley or dill
  - A drizzle of olive oil
  - A sprinkle of nutritional yeast (if tolerated)

Instructions:

1. Heat the avocado oil or ghee in a large pot or Dutch oven over medium heat.
2. Add the diced onion and cook until softened, about 5 minutes.
3. Add the minced garlic and cook for an additional minute, until fragrant.
4. Add the broccoli florets and chopped kale to the pot.
5. Cook for 5-7 minutes, or until the kale has wilted and the broccoli is bright green.
6. Pour in the vegetable broth (or bone broth), thyme, oregano, salt, and pepper.
7. Bring to a boil, then reduce heat and simmer for 10-15 minutes, or until the broccoli is tender.
8. Remove the pot from the heat and carefully transfer the soup to a blender.
9. Blend until smooth and creamy. (Alternatively, you can use an immersion blender directly in the pot.)
10. Return the soup to the pot. If desired, stir in the coconut milk for extra creaminess.
11. Heat gently over low heat, stirring occasionally, until warmed through.
12. Ladle the soup into bowls and garnish with chopped parsley or dill, a drizzle of olive oil, and a sprinkle of nutritional yeast (if tolerated).

Tips:

- For a richer flavor, use homemade bone broth instead of store-bought.
- Feel free to adjust the amount of kale and broccoli to your preference.
- If you don't have fresh herbs, you can use dried herbs, but use half the amount as they are more concentrated.
- Leftover soup can be stored in the refrigerator for up to 5 days or frozen for later.

I love this soup because it's so packed with nutrients and flavor. It's a great way to get my daily dose of greens, and the creamy texture and warm spices make it incredibly comforting. I often make a big batch at the beginning of the week and enjoy it for lunch or dinner throughout the week.

Enjoy this vibrant and nourishing Broccoli and Kale Soup as a healthy and satisfying meal on the AIP diet!

Chicken and Sweet Potato Chowder: A Creamy, AIP-Friendly Comfort

Prep Time: 15 minutes **Cook Time:** 40 minutes **Yields:** 4-6 servings

This creamy and hearty chowder is a delicious and satisfying meal for those following the AIP diet. Tender chicken, sweet potatoes, and aromatic vegetables simmer in a flavorful broth, thickened with creamy coconut milk. This chowder is a comforting and nutritious dish perfect for cooler weather or any time you crave a cozy meal.

Ingredients:

- 2 tablespoons avocado oil or ghee
- 1 large yellow onion, diced
- 2 cloves garlic, minced
- 3 carrots, peeled and chopped
- 3 stalks celery, chopped
- 2 pounds boneless, skinless chicken thighs or breasts, cut into bite-sized pieces
- 4 cups chicken broth (homemade or store-bought)
- 2 medium sweet potatoes, peeled and diced
- 1 teaspoon dried thyme
- 1/2 teaspoon dried rosemary
- 1/4 teaspoon sea salt
- 1/4 teaspoon black pepper
- 1 cup full-fat coconut milk
- Optional add-ins:
    - 1/2 cup chopped parsnips
    - 1/2 cup chopped turnips
    - 1 cup sliced mushrooms
    - 1/4 cup chopped fresh parsley, for garnish

Instructions:

1. Heat the avocado oil or ghee in a large pot or Dutch oven over medium heat.
2. Add the diced onion and cook until softened, about 5 minutes.
3. Add the minced garlic and cook for an additional minute, until fragrant.
4. Then add the carrots and celery and cook for another 5 minutes until softened.
5. Add the chicken pieces and chicken broth to the pot.
6. Bring to a boil, then reduce heat and simmer for 15-20 minutes, or until the chicken is cooked through.
7. Add the sweet potatoes, thyme, rosemary, salt, and pepper to the pot.
8. If desired, add any optional vegetables (parsnips, turnips, or mushrooms).
9. Bring to a simmer and cook for an additional 15-20 minutes, or until the sweet potatoes are tender.
10. Stir in the coconut milk and cook for 5 minutes, or until heated through.
11. Ladle the chowder into bowls and garnish with fresh parsley, if desired.

Tips:

- For a richer flavor, use homemade bone broth made from chicken bones.
- Feel free to adjust the amount and type of vegetables to your preference.
- You can make this recipe in a slow cooker by following the same instructions, but cooking on low for 6-8 hours or high for 3-4 hours.
- If you prefer a thicker chowder, you can mash some of the sweet potatoes against the side of the pot with a fork before serving.
- Leftover chowder can be stored in the refrigerator for up to 5 days or frozen for later.

I love this chowder because it's so comforting and satisfying, especially on a cold day. The creamy coconut milk and the sweetness of the sweet potatoes make it a real treat, and it's always a hit with my family and friends.

Enjoy this delicious and nourishing Chicken and Sweet Potato Chowder as a healthy and satisfying meal on the AIP diet!

AIP Pumpkin Chili: A Warm & Cozy Fall Favorite

Prep Time: 15 minutes **Cook Time:** 30-45 minutes (stovetop) or 4-6 hours (slow cooker) **Yields:** 6-8 servings

This hearty and flavorful chili is a perfect way to warm up on a chilly day while adhering to the AIP diet. The combination of pumpkin puree, ground beef, warming spices, and a touch of sweetness from maple syrup (optional) creates a comforting and nutritious meal that's sure to become a fall favorite.

Ingredients:

- 1 tablespoon avocado oil or ghee
- 1 large yellow onion, diced
- 2 cloves garlic, minced
- 1 pound ground beef (grass-fed, if possible)
- 1 tablespoon chili powder (AIP-compliant, check for nightshades)
- 1 teaspoon ground cumin
- 1/2 teaspoon smoked paprika
- 1/4 teaspoon cayenne pepper (optional, for extra spice)
- 1/4 teaspoon sea salt
- 1/4 teaspoon black pepper
- 1 (15-ounce) can pumpkin puree (NOT pumpkin pie filling)
- 2 cups beef broth (homemade or store-bought)
- 1 tablespoon apple cider vinegar
- 1 tablespoon maple syrup (optional, for a touch of sweetness)

- Optional garnishes:
    - Chopped fresh cilantro
    - Sliced avocado
    - A dollop of coconut milk yogurt (if tolerated)

Instructions:

Stovetop Method:

1. Heat the avocado oil or ghee in a large pot or Dutch oven over medium heat.
2. Add the diced onion and cook until softened, about 5 minutes.
3. Add the minced garlic and cook for an additional minute, until fragrant.
4. Add the ground beef and cook until browned, breaking it up with a spatula as it cooks.
5. Stir in the chili powder, cumin, smoked paprika, cayenne pepper (if using), salt, and pepper.
6. Cook for 1 minute, stirring constantly, until fragrant.
7. Add the pumpkin puree, beef broth, apple cider vinegar, and maple syrup (if using) to the pot.
8. Bring to a simmer and cook for 20-30 minutes, or until the chili has thickened and the flavors have melded.

Slow Cooker Method:

1. Brown the ground beef in a skillet over medium heat, as described in steps 1-3 above.
2. Drain any excess grease.
3. Transfer the browned beef to the slow cooker.
4. Add the remaining ingredients to the slow cooker and stir to combine.
5. Cover and cook on low for 6-8 hours, or on high for 3-4 hours, or until the chili has thickened and the flavors have melded.

Serve: Ladle the chili into bowls and garnish with your favorite toppings.

Tips:

- For a thicker chili, simmer it uncovered for a longer period or add a tablespoon of arrowroot powder or tapioca starch mixed with a little water during the last 15 minutes of cooking.
- Feel free to adjust the amount of spices to your liking.
- If you don't have any bone broth on hand, you can use water instead.
- Leftover chili can be stored in the refrigerator for up to 5 days or frozen for later.

I love making this pumpkin chili on a chilly fall day. It's so comforting and flavorful, and the warm spices make the house smell amazing. It's a great meal for a cozy night in or for sharing with friends and family.

"Good food is good mood." - Unknown

AIP French Onion Soup: Savory Comfort, Simplified

Prep Time: 15 minutes **Cook Time:** 45-60 minutes **Yields:** 4 servings

This comforting and flavorful French Onion Soup is a classic dish reimagined for the AIP diet. While the traditional recipe relies on ingredients like bread and cheese for its signature topping, this version focuses on the essence of the soup: deeply caramelized onions simmered in a rich broth, infused with aromatic herbs. It's a simple yet satisfying meal that's perfect for chilly evenings or when you're craving a taste of French cuisine.

Ingredients:

- 4 large yellow onions, thinly sliced
- 2 tablespoons avocado oil or ghee
- 4 cups beef broth (homemade or store-bought)
- 1 teaspoon dried thyme
- 1/2 teaspoon dried rosemary
- 1/4 teaspoon sea salt
- 1/4 teaspoon black pepper
- Optional garnishes:
    - Chopped fresh parsley or chives
    - A drizzle of olive oil

Instructions:

1. Heat the avocado oil or ghee in a large pot or Dutch oven over medium heat.
2. Add the sliced onions and cook, stirring occasionally, until they are deeply caramelized and golden brown, about 45-60 minutes. This step takes patience, but it's crucial for developing the rich, sweet flavor of the soup.
3. Pour in the beef broth, thyme, rosemary, salt, and pepper.
4. Bring to a boil, then reduce heat and simmer for 15 minutes to allow the flavors to meld.
5. Ladle the soup into bowls and garnish with chopped fresh parsley or chives and a drizzle of olive oil, if desired.

Tips:

- For a richer flavor, use homemade bone broth made from beef bones.
- To speed up the caramelization process, you can add a pinch of baking soda to the onions while they're cooking.
- If you're short on time, you can caramelize the onions in a slow cooker on low for 8-10 hours.
- If you tolerate nightshades, you can add a bay leaf to the soup while it simmers for additional flavor.

I used to love French Onion Soup, but the bread and cheese topping wasn't compatible with my AIP diet. This simplified version is just as satisfying, and I love the intense flavor that comes from the slow-cooked caramelized onions. It's a comforting and delicious meal that I always look forward to.

Enjoy this flavorful and comforting AIP French Onion Soup as a healthy and satisfying meal that's sure to warm you up from the inside out!

Sides

"Healthy food doesn't have to be boring. With a little creativity, you can make delicious and nutritious dishes that satisfy your cravings and nourish your body." - Unknown

AIP Mashed Sweet Potatoes: A Silky & Satisfying Side Dish

Prep Time: 10 minutes **Cook Time:** 20-25 minutes **Yields:** 4 servings

This velvety smooth and flavorful mashed sweet potato dish is a perfect addition to any AIP meal. The creamy texture and subtle sweetness of sweet potatoes are enhanced by the richness of coconut milk and ghee, creating a comforting and satisfying side dish that's packed with nutrients.

Ingredients:

- 2 pounds sweet potatoes, peeled and cubed
- 1/4 cup full-fat coconut milk (or more, for desired consistency)
- 2 tablespoons ghee or avocado oil
- 1/4 teaspoon sea salt
- 1/4 teaspoon black pepper
- Optional add-ins:
    - Pinch of ground cinnamon
    - Pinch of ground nutmeg
    - Chopped fresh herbs (parsley, thyme, or rosemary)

Instructions:

1. Place the cubed sweet potatoes in a large pot and cover with water.
2. Bring to a boil, then reduce heat and simmer until the sweet potatoes are fork-tender, about 15-20 minutes.
3. Drain the sweet potatoes thoroughly and return them to the pot.
4. Mash with a potato masher or fork until smooth.
5. Stir in the coconut milk, ghee, salt, and pepper.
6. If desired, add any optional spices or herbs.
7. If the mashed sweet potatoes are too thick, add a bit more coconut milk until desired consistency is reached.
8. Serve warm as a side dish or enjoy on its own as a light meal.

Tips:

- For a richer flavor, roast the sweet potatoes instead of boiling them. Preheat the oven to 400°F (200°C) and toss the cubed sweet potatoes with avocado oil, salt, and pepper.

- Roast for 20-25 minutes, or until tender and slightly caramelized.
- Feel free to adjust the amount of coconut milk and ghee to your liking. If you prefer a less rich dish, use less fat.
- For a smoother texture, you can use a food processor or immersion blender to mash the sweet potatoes.

I love this mashed sweet potato recipe because it's so simple to make and incredibly versatile. It's a great side dish for chicken, fish, or beef, and it's also delicious on its own with a sprinkle of fresh herbs.

Enjoy this creamy and satisfying Mashed Sweet Potatoes as a healthy and flavorful side dish on the AIP diet!

"Eat your greens!" - Mom

Garlic Green Beans: Simple, Savory, & AIP-Approved

Prep Time: 5 minutes **Cook Time:** 10-15 minutes **Yields:** 4 servings

This simple yet flavorful side dish is a perfect addition to any AIP meal. Fresh green beans are sautéed with garlic and olive oil, creating a delicious and nutritious dish that's packed with vitamins and minerals.

Ingredients:

- 1 pound fresh green beans, trimmed and cut into 1-inch pieces
- 2 tablespoons avocado oil or ghee
- 4 cloves garlic, minced
- 1/2 teaspoon sea salt
- 1/4 teaspoon black pepper
- Optional garnishes:
    - A squeeze of lemon juice
    - Red pepper flakes (for a spicy kick)
    - Chopped fresh herbs (parsley, thyme, or rosemary)

Instructions:

1. If you prefer your green beans to be extra tender, you can blanch them first.
2. Bring a pot of salted water to a boil.
3. Add the green beans and cook for 2-3 minutes, or until bright green and slightly tender.
4. Drain and immediately plunge into an ice bath to stop the cooking process.
5. Heat the avocado oil or ghee in a large skillet over medium heat.
6. Add the minced garlic and cook for 30 seconds, or until fragrant.
7. Add the green beans to the skillet and sauté for 5-7 minutes, or until tender-crisp, stirring occasionally.
8. Season with salt and pepper to taste.
9. Add any optional garnishes, such as a squeeze of lemon juice, red pepper flakes, or chopped fresh herbs.
10. Serve immediately as a delicious and healthy side dish.

Tips:

- For a crispier texture, skip the blanching step and simply sauté the green beans until tender-crisp.
- Feel free to adjust the amount of garlic to your liking.
- If you don't have fresh garlic, you can use garlic powder, but use half the amount as it's more potent.
- Leftover green beans can be stored in an airtight container in the refrigerator for up to 3 days.

I love this recipe because it's so quick and easy to make, and it's a great way to add some extra vegetables to my meals. The garlic and olive oil create a simple yet flavorful combination that complements the fresh green beans perfectly.

Enjoy these delicious and nutritious Garlic Green Beans as a healthy and satisfying side dish on the AIP diet!

"Healthy eating is not about deprivation; it's about nourishment." - Unknown

Roasted Brussels sprouts with Bacon: Crispy, Savory, & AIP-Approved

Prep Time: 10 minutes **Cook Time:** 30-40 minutes **Yields:** 4 servings

This simple yet incredibly flavorful side dish is a perfect addition to any AIP meal. Roasted Brussels sprouts become crispy and caramelized in the oven, while the bacon adds a smoky, savory element. The optional balsamic glaze adds a touch of sweetness and tang for those in the reintroduction phase.

Ingredients:

- 1 pound Brussels sprouts, trimmed and halved
- 4 slices bacon (AIP-compliant, no sugar or nitrates), diced
- 2 tablespoons avocado oil or ghee
- 1/2 teaspoon sea salt
- 1/4 teaspoon black pepper

Optional Glaze (Reintroduction Phase):

- 2 tablespoons balsamic vinegar
- 1 tablespoon honey or maple syrup

Instructions:

1. Preheat your oven to 400°F (200°C). Line a baking sheet with parchment paper.
2. Toss the halved Brussels sprouts with avocado oil or ghee, salt, and pepper in a large bowl.
3. Spread the Brussels sprouts in a single layer on the prepared baking sheet.
4. Sprinkle the diced bacon evenly over the Brussels sprouts.
5. Roast for 20 minutes, or until the Brussels sprouts are starting to soften and brown.
6. **(Reintroduction Phase) Prepare the glaze:** While the Brussels sprouts are roasting, prepare the glaze by whisking together the balsamic vinegar and honey or maple syrup in a small bowl.
7. **(Reintroduction Phase) Add the glaze:** After 20 minutes of roasting, drizzle the balsamic glaze over the Brussels sprouts and bacon. Toss gently to coat.

8. Roast for an additional 10-20 minutes, or until the Brussels sprouts are tender and caramelized, and the bacon is crispy.

Tips:

- For extra crispiness, you can roast the Brussels sprouts for a longer time, but keep a close eye on them to prevent burning.
- Feel free to add other AIP-compliant spices to the Brussels sprouts, such as garlic powder, onion powder, or smoked paprika.
- You can also use leftover cooked bacon for this recipe.

I used to hate Brussels sprouts as a kid, but roasting them with bacon completely changed my mind! The smoky bacon and the caramelized edges of the sprouts create a delicious and irresistible combination that I can't get enough of.

Enjoy these flavorful and crispy Roasted Brussels Sprouts with Bacon as a delicious and satisfying side dish on the AIP diet!

"Eating healthy doesn't have to be boring. With a little creativity, you can make delicious and nutritious dishes that satisfy your cravings and nourish your body." - Unknown

Baked Carrot Fries: A Crispy & Flavorful AIP Snack

Prep Time: 10 minutes **Cook Time:** 25-35 minutes **Yields:** 4 servings

These crispy and flavorful baked carrot fries are a delicious and healthy alternative to traditional French fries, perfect for those following the AIP diet. They're made with simple ingredients and seasoned with warming spices for a satisfying snack or side dish.

Ingredients:

- 4 large carrots, peeled and cut into 1/4-inch thick sticks
- 2 tablespoons avocado oil or ghee
- 1/4 cup arrowroot flour or tapioca flour
- 1/2 teaspoon garlic powder
- 1/2 teaspoon onion powder
- 1/4 teaspoon paprika
- 1/4 teaspoon sea salt
- 1/4 teaspoon black pepper

Instructions:

1. Preheat your oven to 400°F (200°C). Line a baking sheet with parchment paper.

2. In a large bowl, toss the carrot sticks with avocado oil or ghee until evenly coated.
3. In a separate bowl, combine the arrowroot flour or tapioca flour, garlic powder, onion powder, paprika, salt, and pepper.
4. Sprinkle the mixture over the carrots and toss until evenly coated.
5. Arrange the carrot sticks in a single layer on the prepared baking sheet, making sure they don't overlap.
6. Bake for 25-35 minutes, or until golden brown and tender, flipping halfway through.
7. Let cool slightly before serving.
8. Enjoy as a snack or side dish with your favorite AIP-compliant dipping sauce.

Tips:

- For extra crispy fries, you can increase the baking time by a few minutes, but keep a close eye on them to prevent burning.
- Feel free to experiment with different spices to create your own unique flavor combinations. Try adding a pinch of cumin, coriander, or chili powder for a spicier kick.
- If you don't have arrowroot flour or tapioca flour, you can omit it, but the fries may not be as crispy.

I love making these carrot fries for my kids as a healthy alternative to French fries. They're always a hit, and I feel good knowing that they're getting a serving of vegetables in a fun and delicious way.

Enjoy these flavorful and crispy Baked Carrot Fries as a healthy and satisfying snack or side dish on the AIP diet!

AIP Broccoli Salad: Crunchy, Creamy, and Refreshing

Prep Time: 10 minutes **Chill Time:** 30 minutes (optional) **Yields:** 4 servings

This vibrant and flavorful broccoli salad is a refreshing and healthy side dish or snack for those following the AIP diet. Crisp broccoli florets are tossed with a creamy and tangy dressing made with avocado, lemon juice, and herbs, and studded with sweet dried cranberries for a burst of flavor and texture.

Ingredients:

- For the Salad:
    - 4 cups broccoli florets, chopped into bite-sized pieces
    - 1/2 cup dried cranberries (unsweetened, no sulfites)
- For the Avocado Dressing:

- 1 ripe avocado, pitted and peeled
- 2 tablespoons lemon juice
- 2 tablespoons olive oil
- 1/4 cup chopped fresh parsley
- 1/4 teaspoon garlic powder
- 1/4 teaspoon onion powder
- 1/4 teaspoon sea salt
- 1/4 teaspoon black pepper

Instructions:

1. In a food processor or blender, combine all the dressing ingredients and blend until smooth and creamy.
2. If the mixture is too thick, add a tablespoon of water at a time until desired consistency is reached.
3. In a large bowl, combine the chopped broccoli florets and dried cranberries.
4. Pour the avocado dressing over the broccoli and cranberries. Toss gently to coat.
5. You can enjoy the salad immediately, but it's best to chill it in the refrigerator for at least 30 minutes to allow the flavors to meld.

Tips:

- For a spicier kick, add a pinch of cayenne pepper or a dash of hot sauce to the dressing.
- Feel free to add other AIP-compliant ingredients to the salad, such as chopped bacon (cooked until crispy), diced red onion, or chopped celery.
- You can substitute other AIP-compliant dried fruits, such as chopped dates or apricots, for the cranberries.

I love this broccoli salad because it's so easy to make and always a crowd-pleaser. The creamy avocado dressing is a delicious and healthy alternative to traditional mayonnaise-based dressings, and the dried cranberries add a burst of sweetness that balances the savory flavors. It's a perfect side dish for barbecues, potlucks, or a light lunch.

Enjoy this refreshing and flavorful AIP Broccoli Salad as a healthy and satisfying addition to your meal plan!

AIP Mashed Cauliflower: A Cloud of Comfort (Dairy-Free & Delicious)

Prep Time: 5 minutes **Cook Time:** 15 minutes **Yields:** 4 servings

This light and fluffy mashed cauliflower is a delicious and nutritious alternative to mashed potatoes on the AIP diet. It's incredibly simple to make, packed with vitamins and minerals, and can be customized with your favorite herbs and spices.

Ingredients:

- 1 large head of cauliflower, cut into florets
- 1/4 cup full-fat coconut milk (or more, for desired consistency)
- 2 tablespoons ghee or avocado oil
- 1/2 teaspoon garlic powder
- 1/4 teaspoon onion powder
- 1/4 teaspoon sea salt
- 1/4 teaspoon black pepper
- Optional garnishes:
    - Chopped fresh chives or parsley
    - A drizzle of olive oil

Instructions:

1. Place the cauliflower florets in a steamer basket over a pot of boiling water or directly in the pot.
2. Cook until tender, about 10-15 minutes.
3. Drain the cauliflower thoroughly and transfer it to a large bowl.
4. Mash the cauliflower with a potato masher or fork until smooth.
5. Alternatively, you can use a food processor or immersion blender, but be careful not to over-process, as this can make the cauliflower gummy.
6. Stir in the coconut milk, ghee or avocado oil, garlic powder, onion powder, salt, and pepper.
7. Mix well until combined.
8. If the mashed cauliflower is too thick, add a bit more coconut milk until you reach your desired consistency.
9. Serve warm, garnished with chopped fresh chives or parsley and a drizzle of olive oil, if desired.

Tips:

- For a richer flavor, roast the cauliflower florets instead of steaming or boiling them. Preheat the oven to 400°F (200°C) and toss the florets with avocado oil, salt, and pepper. Roast for 20-25 minutes, or until tender and slightly browned.
- Feel free to experiment with different herbs and spices, such as rosemary, thyme, or sage.
- You can also add other AIP-compliant ingredients to the mashed cauliflower, such as roasted garlic, caramelized onions, or chopped bacon (cooked until crispy).
- Leftover mashed cauliflower can be stored in an airtight container in the refrigerator for up to 3 days.

I used to think mashed potatoes were the only way to enjoy creamy, comforting mashed vegetables, but this AIP mashed cauliflower recipe has become a new favorite. It's so easy to make, and the creamy texture and savory flavors are incredibly satisfying.

Enjoy this delicious and healthy Mashed Cauliflower as a lighter and AIP-friendly alternative to mashed potatoes!

Sautéed Kale with Garlic: A Nutrient-Rich AIP Side Dish

Prep Time: 5 minutes **Cook Time:** 10 minutes **Yields:** 4 servings

This simple yet flavorful side dish is a delicious way to enjoy the nutritional benefits of kale on the AIP diet. The hearty greens are sautéed with garlic and olive oil, creating a tender and flavorful dish that's perfect for any meal.

Ingredients:

- 1 bunch of kale, stems removed and chopped
- 2 tablespoons avocado oil or ghee
- 4 cloves garlic, minced
- 1/2 teaspoon sea salt
- 1/4 teaspoon black pepper
- Optional additions:
    - A squeeze of lemon juice
    - Red pepper flakes (for a spicy kick)

Instructions:

1. Heat the avocado oil or ghee in a large skillet over medium heat.
2. Add the minced garlic and cook for 30 seconds, or until fragrant, being careful not to burn it.
3. Add the chopped kale to the skillet and sauté for 5-7 minutes, or until wilted and tender, stirring occasionally.
4. Season with salt and pepper to taste.
5. Add a squeeze of lemon juice and red pepper flakes, if desired.
6. Serve immediately as a delicious and healthy side dish.

Tips:

- For a more tender kale, you can massage the leaves with the oil and salt for a few minutes before adding them to the skillet.
- Feel free to adjust the amount of garlic to your liking.
- If you don't have fresh garlic, you can use garlic powder, but use half the amount as it's more potent.
- Leftover kale can be stored in an airtight container in the refrigerator for up to 3 days.

I used to think kale was too tough and bitter, but this recipe has completely changed my mind. Sautéing it with garlic and olive oil softens it up and brings out its natural sweetness. It's a simple yet flavorful dish that I now enjoy regularly.

Enjoy this delicious and nutritious Sautéed Kale with Garlic as a healthy and satisfying side dish on the AIP diet!

Desserts & Sweets

"Healthy eating is not about deprivation; it's about nourishment." – Unknown

AIP Coconut Flour Brownies: Fudgy, Decadent, and Healing

Prep Time: 10 minutes **Cook Time:** 20-25 minutes **Yields:** 8-10 brownies

These fudgy and intensely chocolatey brownies are a delicious treat that's surprisingly compliant with the AIP diet. Made with coconut flour, cocoa powder, honey, and other wholesome ingredients, they're a guilt-free indulgence that satisfies your sweet tooth while nourishing your body.

Ingredients:

- 1/2 cup coconut flour
- 1/2 cup cocoa powder
- 1/2 teaspoon baking soda
- 1/4 teaspoon sea salt
- 1/2 cup coconut oil, melted and slightly cooled
- 1/2 cup honey or maple syrup
- 3 large eggs
- 1 teaspoon vanilla extract
- 1/2 cup chopped walnuts or pecans (optional)
- 1/4 cup AIP-compliant chocolate chips (optional)

Instructions:

1. Preheat your oven to 350°F (175°C). Line an 8x8 inch baking pan with parchment paper.
2. In a medium bowl, whisk together the coconut flour, cocoa powder, baking soda, and salt.
3. In a separate bowl, whisk together the melted coconut oil, honey or maple syrup, eggs, and vanilla extract until smooth.
4. Gradually add the dry ingredients to the wet ingredients, whisking until just combined. Do not overmix.
5. Fold in the chopped nuts and/or chocolate chips, if using.
6. Pour the batter into the prepared baking pan and spread evenly. Bake for 20-25 minutes, or until a toothpick inserted into the center comes out clean.
7. Let the brownies cool completely in the pan before cutting into squares.

Tips:

- Don't overmix the batter, as this can result in dense and rubbery brownies.
- For a fudgier texture, underbake the brownies slightly. The center should still be a bit soft when you take them out of the oven.
- If you don't have parchment paper, you can grease and flour the baking pan instead.

- Store the brownies in an airtight container at room temperature for up to 3 days or in the refrigerator for up to 5 days.

I used to think that brownies were off-limits on the AIP diet, but this recipe proved me wrong! These coconut flour brownies are so rich, fudgy, and satisfying that I can hardly believe they're actually good for me. They're perfect for satisfying my chocolate cravings without any guilt.

Indulge in these delicious and nutritious AIP Coconut Flour Brownies as a sweet and satisfying treat that won't compromise your health goals.

AIP Coconut Flour Brownies: Fudgy, Decadent, and Healing

Prep Time: 10 minutes **Cook Time:** 20-25 minutes **Yields:** 8-10 brownies

These fudgy and intensely chocolatey brownies are a delicious treat that's surprisingly compliant with the AIP diet. Made with coconut flour, cocoa powder, honey, and other wholesome ingredients, they're a guilt-free indulgence that satisfies your sweet tooth while nourishing your body.

Ingredients:

- 1/2 cup coconut flour
- 1/2 cup cocoa powder
- 1/2 teaspoon baking soda
- 1/4 teaspoon sea salt
- 1/2 cup coconut oil, melted and slightly cooled
- 1/2 cup honey or maple syrup
- 3 large eggs
- 1 teaspoon vanilla extract
- 1/2 cup chopped walnuts or pecans (optional)
- 1/4 cup AIP-compliant chocolate chips (optional)

Instructions:

1. Preheat your oven to 350°F (175°C). Line an 8x8 inch baking pan with parchment paper.
2. In a medium bowl, whisk together the coconut flour, cocoa powder, baking soda, and salt.
3. In a separate bowl, whisk together the melted coconut oil, honey or maple syrup, eggs, and vanilla extract until smooth.
4. Gradually add the dry ingredients to the wet ingredients, whisking until just combined. Do not overmix.
5. Fold in the chopped nuts and/or chocolate chips, if using.
6. Pour the batter into the prepared baking pan and spread evenly.
7. Bake for 20-25 minutes, or until a toothpick inserted into the center comes out clean.

8. Let the brownies cool completely in the pan before cutting into squares.

Tips:

- Don't overmix the batter, as this can result in dense and rubbery brownies.
- For a fudgier texture, underbake the brownies slightly. The center should still be a bit soft when you take them out of the oven.
- If you don't have parchment paper, you can grease and flour the baking pan instead.
- Store the brownies in an airtight container at room temperature for up to 3 days or in the refrigerator for up to 5 days.

I used to think that brownies were off-limits on the AIP diet, but this recipe proved me wrong! These coconut flour brownies are so rich, fudgy, and satisfying that I can hardly believe they're actually good for me. They're perfect for satisfying my chocolate cravings without any guilt.

Indulge in these delicious and nutritious AIP Coconut Flour Brownies as a sweet and satisfying treat that won't compromise your health goals.

AIP Banana Nice Cream: A Naturally Sweet & Creamy Frozen Treat

Prep Time: 5 minutes (plus freezing time)
Blend Time: 5 minutes **Yields:** 2 servings

This simple and delicious Banana Nice Cream is a healthy and satisfying alternative to ice cream, perfect for those following the AIP diet. Made with just one ingredient – frozen bananas – it's naturally sweet, creamy, and packed with nutrients. It's a guilt-free dessert that's perfect for cooling down on a hot day or satisfying your sweet tooth.

Ingredients:

- 4 ripe bananas, peeled and sliced (preferably frozen overnight)

Optional Add-ins:

- 1/4 cup full-fat coconut milk (for extra creaminess)
- 1/2 teaspoon vanilla extract
- Pinch of cinnamon or nutmeg
- Other AIP-compliant toppings like berries, shredded coconut, or chopped nuts (if reintroduced)

Instructions:

1. Peel and slice the bananas.
2. Spread the slices out on a baking sheet lined with parchment paper and freeze for at least 4 hours, or preferably overnight.

3. Add the frozen banana slices to a food processor or high-powered blender.
4. If using, add the coconut milk, vanilla extract, and spices.
5. Blend the mixture until it's smooth and creamy, scraping down the sides of the blender as needed.
6. You may need to add a splash of water or coconut milk to help it blend if it's too thick.
7. Enjoy the Banana Nice Cream immediately for a soft-serve consistency, or freeze for an hour or two for a firmer texture.

Tips:

- For a richer flavor, use overripe bananas with brown spots.
- Feel free to experiment with different flavors by adding other AIP-compliant fruits, such as berries, mango, or pineapple.
- You can also add a scoop of AIP-compliant protein powder for an extra boost of nutrients.

I stumbled upon this recipe when I was craving ice cream on the AIP diet, and I was amazed at how delicious and satisfying it was. It's become my go-to dessert on hot summer days, and I love experimenting with different flavor combinations.

Indulge in this creamy and delicious Banana Nice Cream as a healthy and satisfying treat on the AIP diet!

Mango Sorbet: A Tropical Twist on a Refreshing Treat (AIP-Friendly)

Prep Time: 10 minutes (plus freezing time) **Blend Time:** 5 minutes **Yields:** 4 servings

This vibrant and refreshing mango sorbet is a delightful treat for those following the AIP diet. Made with just a few simple ingredients, it's naturally sweet, bursting with tropical flavor, and completely dairy-free. Perfect for cooling down on a hot day or satisfying your sweet tooth in a healthy way.

Ingredients:

- 3 cups frozen mango chunks
- 1/4 cup honey or maple syrup (adjust to taste)
- 2 tablespoons lime juice (freshly squeezed)
- 1/4 cup water (optional, for a smoother consistency)

Instructions:

1. If using fresh mangoes, peel, pit, and chop them into chunks.
2. Spread the chunks on a baking sheet lined with parchment paper

and freeze for at least 4 hours or overnight.
3. Add the frozen mango chunks, honey or maple syrup, lime juice, and water (if using) to a food processor or high-powered blender.
4. Blend the mixture until it's smooth and creamy, scraping down the sides of the blender as needed. You may need to add a splash of water to help it blend if it's too thick.
5. For a soft-serve consistency, enjoy the sorbet immediately.
6. For a firmer texture, transfer the mixture to a freezer-safe container and freeze for 1-2 hours before serving.

Tips:
- For a more intense mango flavor, use ripe mangoes that are sweet and fragrant.
- If you don't have fresh mangoes, you can use frozen mango chunks.
- Feel free to adjust the amount of honey or maple syrup to your liking. If the mangoes are very sweet, you may need less sweetener.
- If you don't have lime juice, you can use lemon juice instead.
- For a fun twist, try adding a pinch of chili powder or cayenne pepper to the sorbet for a touch of heat.

I love making this mango sorbet in the summer when mangoes are in season. It's so refreshing and flavorful, and it's a great way to cool down on a hot day. My kids love it too, and it's a healthy alternative to sugary store-bought treats.

Indulge in this refreshing and delicious Mango Sorbet as a healthy and satisfying treat on the AIP diet!

AIP Apple Crisp: Warm & Comforting Autumnal Bliss

Prep Time: 15 minutes **Cook Time:** 35-40 minutes **Yields:** 6-8 servings

This warm and comforting apple crisp is a delicious and satisfying dessert that's perfect for the AIP diet. Made with sweet and tart apples, a cinnamon-spiced crumble topping, and a touch of honey, it's a guilt-free indulgence that's sure to become a fall favorite.

Ingredients:

For the Apple Filling:

- 6-8 apples (Honeycrisp, Granny Smith, or a mix), peeled, cored, and sliced
- 1/4 cup lemon juice
- 1 tablespoon arrowroot starch or tapioca flour
- 1/4 cup honey or maple syrup
- 1 tablespoon cinnamon
- 1/4 teaspoon nutmeg

- 1/4 teaspoon sea salt

For the Crumble Topping:

- 1 cup shredded coconut (unsweetened)
- 1/2 cup almond flour
- 1/4 cup tapioca flour (or arrowroot flour)
- 1/4 cup coconut oil, melted
- 2 tablespoons honey or maple syrup
- 1 teaspoon cinnamon

Instructions:

1. Preheat your oven to 375°F (190°C). Grease an 8x8 inch baking dish.
2. In a large bowl, toss the sliced apples with lemon juice, arrowroot starch (or tapioca flour), honey or maple syrup, cinnamon, nutmeg, and salt.
3. : In a separate bowl, combine the shredded coconut, almond flour, tapioca flour (or arrowroot flour), melted coconut oil, honey or maple syrup, and cinnamon.
4. Use your fingers to mix until the mixture is crumbly.
5. Spread the apple filling evenly in the prepared baking dish.
6. Crumble the topping mixture over the apples.
7. Bake for 35-40 minutes, or until the apples are tender and the topping is golden brown.
8. Let cool slightly before serving.
9. Enjoy warm with a dollop of coconut whipped cream (if desired).

Tips:

- For a richer flavor, use a mix of sweet and tart apples, such as Honeycrisp and Granny Smith.
- Feel free to adjust the amount of honey or maple syrup to your liking. If the apples are very sweet, you may need less sweetener.
- You can substitute other AIP-compliant sweeteners, such as date paste or mashed banana, for the honey or maple syrup.
- If you're sensitive to nuts, you can omit the almond flour or replace it with another AIP-compliant flour, such as tigernut flour.

I have fond memories of making apple crisp with my grandmother when I was a child. This AIP-compliant version brings back those warm and fuzzy feelings, and it's just as delicious as I remember. It's a perfect dessert for cozy fall evenings or holiday gatherings.

Enjoy this delicious and comforting AIP Apple Crisp as a healthy and satisfying treat!

AIP Chocolate Avocado Pudding: Decadent & Guilt-Free

Prep Time: 5 minutes **Chill Time:** 30 minutes (optional) **Yields:** 2 servings

This luscious and velvety pudding is a chocolate lover's dream come true, even on the AIP diet! Avocado provides a rich and creamy base, while cocoa powder delivers a deep chocolate flavor. It's a surprisingly healthy dessert that's packed with nutrients and free of refined sugar and dairy.

Ingredients:

- 1 ripe avocado, pitted and peeled
- 1/4 cup cocoa powder
- 1/4 cup honey or maple syrup (adjust to taste)
- 1/4 cup full-fat coconut milk (or more, for desired consistency)
- 1 teaspoon vanilla extract
- Pinch of sea salt
- Optional toppings: shredded coconut, berries, chopped nuts (if reintroduced)

Instructions:

1. In a food processor or blender, combine all ingredients and blend until smooth and creamy.
2. Taste and adjust sweetness as needed.
3. Chill for at least 30 minutes before serving (optional).
4. Garnish with your favorite AIP-compliant toppings and enjoy!

AIP Coconut Milk Ice Cream: Tropical & Refreshing

Prep Time: 10 minutes (plus freezing time) **Freeze Time:** 4-6 hours **Yields:** 4 servings

This creamy and refreshing ice cream is a delightful treat on the AIP diet. Made with just a few simple ingredients, it's a delicious and dairy-free way to cool down and satisfy your sweet tooth.

Ingredients:

- 1 (14-ounce) can full-fat coconut milk
- 1/2 cup honey or maple syrup (adjust to taste)
- 1 teaspoon vanilla extract
- Pinch of sea salt

Instructions:

1. Chill the coconut milk in the refrigerator for at least 8 hours, or overnight.
2. Scoop the thickened cream from the top of the can into a mixing bowl.
3. Add honey or maple syrup, vanilla extract, and salt. Beat with an electric mixer until light and fluffy.
4. Pour the mixture into a freezer-safe container and freeze for at least 4 hours, or until solid.

AIP Pumpkin Spice Muffins: Warm & Cozy Fall Treats

Prep Time: 15 minutes **Cook Time:** 20-25 minutes **Yields:** 12 muffins

These moist and flavorful muffins are a perfect AIP-compliant way to enjoy the comforting flavors of fall. Made with pumpkin puree, warming spices, and almond flour, they're a delicious and nutritious snack or breakfast option.

Ingredients:

- 1 1/2 cups almond flour
- 1/2 cup tapioca flour (or arrowroot flour)
- 1/4 teaspoon baking soda
- 1 teaspoon pumpkin pie spice
- 1/2 teaspoon ground cinnamon
- 1/4 teaspoon sea salt
- 1 cup pumpkin puree
- 1/2 cup honey or maple syrup
- 1/4 cup coconut oil, melted
- 2 large eggs
- 1 teaspoon vanilla extract

Instructions:

1. Preheat oven to 350°F (175°C). Line a muffin tin with paper liners.

2. In a large bowl, whisk together the almond flour, tapioca flour, baking soda, pumpkin pie spice, cinnamon, and salt.
3. In a separate bowl, whisk together the pumpkin puree, honey or maple syrup, coconut oil, eggs, and vanilla extract.
4. Add the wet ingredients to the dry ingredients and mix until just combined. Do not overmix.
5. Divide the batter evenly among the prepared muffin cups.
6. Bake for 20-25 minutes, or until a toothpick inserted into the center comes out clean.
7. Let the muffins cool in the pan for a few minutes before transferring to a wire rack to cool completely.

I've always loved the flavors of pumpkin and spice, and these AIP muffins allow me to enjoy them without any guilt. They're perfect for a quick breakfast or a satisfying snack, and they always remind me of cozy fall days.

Enjoy these delicious AIP treats as you nourish your body and satisfy your sweet tooth!

Strawberry Chia Seed Pudding: A Refreshing & Nutritious AIP Treat

Prep Time: 5 minutes **Chill Time:** At least 2 hours, or overnight **Yields:** 2 servings

This simple and delicious chia seed pudding is a refreshing and healthy snack or dessert, perfect for those following the AIP diet. Chia seeds are packed with fiber, omega-3 fatty acids, and antioxidants, while strawberries add natural sweetness and vibrant flavor. The coconut milk provides a creamy base and a hint of tropical taste.

Ingredients:

- 1/2 cup full-fat coconut milk (from a can or carton)
- 1/4 cup water
- 1/4 cup chia seeds
- 1/2 teaspoon vanilla extract
- Pinch of sea salt
- 1 cup sliced strawberries
- Optional toppings: shredded coconut, chopped nuts (if reintroduced), a drizzle of honey or maple syrup

Instructions:

1. In a jar or bowl, whisk together the coconut milk, water, chia seeds, vanilla extract, and salt.
2. Cover and refrigerate for at least 2 hours, or preferably overnight, to allow the chia seeds to absorb the liquid and thicken into a pudding-like consistency.
3. When ready to serve, layer the chia seed pudding with sliced

strawberries in glasses or bowls. Top with shredded coconut, chopped nuts (if reintroduced), or a drizzle of honey or maple syrup, if desired.

Tips:

- For a smoother pudding, you can blend the chia seeds with the coconut milk and water before chilling.
- Feel free to use other AIP-compliant fruits, such as blueberries, raspberries, or chopped mango, instead of strawberries.
- You can also add a scoop of AIP-compliant protein powder to the pudding for an extra boost of nutrients.

AIP Carrot Cake Muffins: Warm & Spiced Treats

Prep Time: 15 minutes **Cook Time:** 20-25 minutes **Yields:** 12 muffins

These moist and flavorful muffins are a delicious and AIP-compliant way to enjoy the comforting flavors of carrot cake. Made with almond flour, shredded carrots, warming spices, and sweetened with coconut sugar, they're a healthy and satisfying snack or breakfast option.

Ingredients:

- 1 1/2 cups almond flour
- 1/2 cup tapioca flour (or arrowroot flour)
- 1/4 cup coconut sugar
- 1 teaspoon baking soda
- 1/2 teaspoon ground cinnamon
- 1/4 teaspoon ground nutmeg
- 1/4 teaspoon ground ginger
- 1/4 teaspoon sea salt
- 1 cup shredded carrots
- 1/2 cup unsweetened applesauce
- 1/4 cup coconut oil, melted
- 2 large eggs
- 1 teaspoon vanilla extract
- Optional add-ins: raisins, chopped dates, chopped walnuts (if reintroduced)

Instructions:

1. Preheat your oven to 350°F (175°C).
2. Line a muffin tin with paper liners.
3. In a large bowl, whisk together the almond flour, tapioca flour, coconut sugar, baking soda, cinnamon, nutmeg, ginger, and salt.
4. In a separate bowl, whisk together the shredded carrots, applesauce, melted coconut oil, eggs, and vanilla extract.
5. Add the wet ingredients to the dry ingredients and mix until just combined.
6. Do not overmix.
7. Fold in the raisins, dates, or walnuts, if using.

8. Divide the batter evenly among the prepared muffin cups.
9. Bake for 20-25 minutes, or until a toothpick inserted into the center comes out clean.
10. Let the muffins cool in the pan for a few minutes before transferring to a wire rack to cool completely.

Tips:

- If the batter is too thick, add a tablespoon or two of water or coconut milk.
- Feel free to adjust the amount of spices to your liking.
- Store the muffins in an airtight container at room temperature for up to 3 days or in the refrigerator for up to 5 days.

I love these carrot cake muffins because they're a healthier take on a classic treat. They're perfect for satisfying my sweet tooth without any guilt, and they always remind me of cozy fall days.

Enjoy these delicious AIP treats as you nourish your body and satisfy your sweet tooth!

Printed in Great Britain
by Amazon